strengthen me according to thy word

one year daily [...] [...]dents

QuietTime

QuietTime
one year daily devotional for students

Word of Life Local Church Ministries
A division of Word of Life Fellowship, Inc.
> Joe Jordan – Executive Director
> Don Lough – Director
> Jack Wyrtzen & Harry Bollback – Founders
> Mike Calhoun – VP of Local Church Ministries

USA
P.O. Box 600
Schroon Lake, NY 12870
talk@wol.org
1-888-932-5827

Web Address: www.wol.org

Canada
RR#8/Owen Sound
ON, Canada N4K 5W4
LCM@wol.ca
1-800-461-3503 or
(519) 376-3516

Publisher's Acknowledgements

Writers and Contributors:

Bobby Barton	Nehemiah, Acts (Chapters 1-12)
Rex Briant	Psalms, Leviticus
Wayne Brown	Ezra, Haggai
Anthony Crumley	Mark
Vince Estill	Proverbs
Cory Fehr	1 Timothy, 1,2,3 John
Andy Grenier	Galatians, Acts (Chapters 13-end)
Joe and Gloria Phillips	Colossians
John Sweat	Numbers, Ruth
Matt Walls	1 & 2 Thessalonians, 2 Peter, Jude

Editor: Dale Flynn
Curriculum Manager: Don Reichard
Cover and page design: Boire Design

ISBN - 978-1-931235-80-8
Printed in the United States of America

Helpful Hints For a Daily QuietTime

The purpose of this Quiet Time is to meet the needs of spiritual growth in the life of the Christian in such a way that they learn the art of conducting their own personal investigation into the Bible. Consider the following helpful hints:

1 Give priority in choosing your quiet time. This will vary with each individual in accordance with his own circumstances. The time you choose must:
- have top priority over everything else
- be the quietest time possible.
- be a convenient time of the day or night.
- be consistently observed each day.

2 Give attention to the procedure suggested for you to follow. Include the following items.
- Read God's Word.
- Mark your Bible as you read. Here are some suggestions that might be helpful:
  - a. After you read the passage put an exclamation mark next to the verses you completely understand.
  - b. Put a question mark next to verses you do not understand.
  - c. Put an arrow pointing upward next to encouraging verses.
  - d. Put an arrow pointing downward next to verses which weigh us down in our spiritual race.
  - e. Put a star next to verses containing important truths or major points.
- Meditate on what you have read (In one sentence, write the main thought). Here are some suggestions as guidelines for meditating on God's Word:

a. Look at the selected passage from God's point of view.

b. Though we encourage quiet time in the morning, some people arrange to have their quiet time at the end of their day. God emphasizes that we need to go to sleep meditating on His Word. "My soul shall be satisfied and my mouth shall praise thee with joyful lips: when I remember thee upon my bed, and meditating on thee in the night watches" (Psalm 63:5,6).

c. Deuteronomy 6:7 lists routine things you do each day during which you should concentrate on the portion of Scripture for that day:

— when you sit in your house (meals and relaxation)
— when you walk in the way (to and from school or work)
— when you lie down (before going to sleep at night)
— when you rise up (getting ready for the day)

☐ Apply some truth to your life. (Use first person pronouns I, me, my, mine). If you have difficulty in finding an application for your life, think of yourself as a Bible SPECTator and ask yourself the following questions.

S – is there any sin for me to forsake?

P – is there any promise for me to claim?

E – is there any example for me to follow?

C – is there any command for me to obey?

T – is there anything to be thankful for today?

☐ Pray for specific things (Use the prayer sheets found in the My Prayer Journal section).

3 Be sure to fill out your quiet time sheets. This will really help you remember the things the Lord brings to your mind.

4 Purpose to share with someone else each day something you gained from your quiet time. This can be a real blessing for them as well as for you.

Step by step through your Quiet Time

The Quiet Time for Students will help you have a special time each day with the Lord. The daily passages are organized so that you cover every book of the Bible in six years. All word of Life Quiet Times use the same daily passage for all ages so families, small groups, or even entire Churches can encourage each other from the Word of God.

The following examples will walk you through the steps to take to have a daily quiet time.

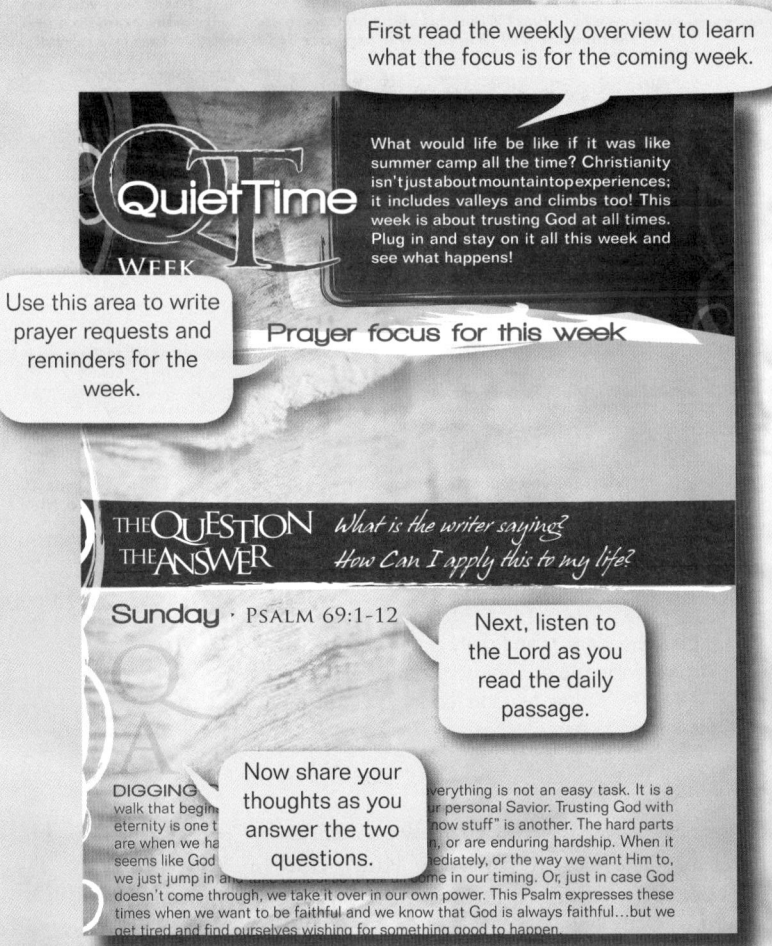

First read the weekly overview to learn what the focus is for the coming week.

QuietTime

WEEK

What would life be like if it was like summer camp all the time? Christianity isn't just about mountaintop experiences; it includes valleys and climbs too! This week is about trusting God at all times. Plug in and stay on it all this week and see what happens!

Use this area to write prayer requests and reminders for the week.

Prayer focus for this week

THE QUESTION *What is the writer saying?*
THE ANSWER *How Can I apply this to my life?*

Sunday · PSALM 69:1-12

Next, listen to the Lord as you read the daily passage.

Now share your thoughts as you answer the two questions.

DIGGING ... everything is not an easy task. It is a walk that begin... ur personal Savior. Trusting God with eternity is one t... now stuff" is another. The hard parts are when we ha... n, or are enduring hardship. When it seems like God ... ediately, or the way we want Him to, we just jump in a... ome in our timing. Or, just in case God doesn't come through, we take it over in our own power. This Psalm expresses these times when we want to be faithful and we know that God is always faithful...but we get tired and find ourselves wishing for something good to happen.

Monday · PSALM 69:13-21

DIGGING DEEPER · Imagine what it would be like to have no hope at all. Consider the thought of not having a relationship with Jesus Christ. It's amazing how [...] to forget what it was like [...] on. As a [...] God, even the deepest and [...] d's love [...] children. God is faithful eve[...] t is His [...] r to deliver what He has pr[...] reading [...] David is at the edge of total loss, but he k[...] e won't go down, only [...] God is faithful.

[...] would it be like to be lost again? What is it that makes you need [...] the most? When does God hear from you? Is it during exam time and in tough trials? Maybe that's why your life is always a test or a crisis!

> Take time to read the Digging Deeper commentary for additional insights on the text.

> Consider these questions as you begin your prayer time.

Tuesday · PSALM 69:22-36

DIGGING DEEPER · If you were shopping for a Christmas gift for God, what do you think you would get Him? Imagine trying to get something for someone that already has everything! Many of us think that God has this list of things He wants and that we are supposed to try and fill His shopping list. According to today's Psalm, in vv. 30-31, David has come to understand that God is not looking for something—He just wants us. God seeks the praise of His people. God seeks to be glorified through your life. All God wants is your praise, worship, and a surrendered life.

What do you think God considers a worthy offering from you today? Have you surrendered your life to God? What could you praise Him for today?

47

> Use the weekly and daily prayer pages in the front of the Quiet Time to organize your prayer time as God leads you.

Give ear to my words, O LORD, consider my meditation. Hearken unto the voice of my cry, my King, and my God: for unto thee will I pray. My voice shalt thou hear in the morning, O LORD; in the morning will I direct my prayer unto thee, and will look up.

Psalm 5:1-3

My Personal
Prayer Journal

Family

Christian Friends

Unsaved Friends

Missionaries

Family

Christian Friends

Unsaved Friends

Missionaries

Family

Christian Friends

Unsaved Friends

Missionaries

Family

Christian Friends

Unsaved Friends

Missionaries

Family

Christian Friends

Unsaved Friends

Missionaries

Family

Christian Friends

Unsaved Friends

Missionaries

Family

Christian Friends

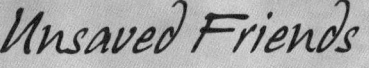

Unsaved Friends

Missionaries

Praise List

Date / Answer

Praise List

Date / Answer

Praise List

Date / Answer

Praise List

Date / Answer

Praise List

Date / Answer

Something for Everyone

Some people just can't get enough! That is why we have several dimensions in the Word of Life Quiet Time. Along with the daily reading, content and application questions for each day, two reading programs are given to help you understand the Bible better. Choose one or both.

Reading Through the New Testament Four Times In One Year

Turn the page and discover a schedule that takes you through the New Testament four times in one year. This is a great method to help you see the correlation of the Gospels and other New Testament books.

Reading Through the Whole Bible In One Year

Turn another page and find a program of several pages that will guide you through a chronological reading of the entire Bible. Follow this schedule and you will move from Genesis through Revelation in one year.

The Choice is Up to You

Whether you have a short quiet time, a quiet time with more scripture reading or one with a mini-Bible study each day, we trust your time with God will draw you closer to Him in every area of your life.

Read through the new testament four times in one year

Weeks 1-13

- ☑ Matthew 1-3
- ☑ Matthew 4-6
- ☑ Matthew 7-9
- ☑ Matt. 10-12
- ☑ Matt. 13-15
- ☑ Matt. 16-18
- ☑ Matt. 19-21
- ☑ Matt. 22-24
- ☑ Matt. 25-26
- ☑ Matt. 27-28
- ☑ Mark 1-3
- ☑ Mark 4-5
- ☑ Mark 6-8
- ☑ Mark 9-11
- ☑ Mark 12-14
- ☑ Mark 15-16
- ☑ Luke 1-2
- ☑ Luke 3-5
- ☑ Luke 6-7
- ☑ Luke 8-9
- ☑ Luke 10-11
- ☑ Luke 12-14
- ☑ Luke 15-17
- ☑ Luke 18-20
- ☑ Luke 21-22
- ☑ Luke 23-24
- ☑ John 1-3
- ☑ John 4-5
- ☑ John 6-7
- ☑ John 8-10
- ☑ John 11-12
- ☑ John 13-15
- ☑ John 16-18
- ☑ John 19-21
- ☑ Acts 1-3
- ☑ Acts 4-6
- ☑ Acts 7-8
- ☑ Acts 9-11
- ☑ Acts 12-15
- ☑ Acts 16-18
- ☑ Acts 19-21
- ☑ Acts 22-24
- ☑ Acts 25-26
- ☑ Acts 27-28
- ☐ Romans 1-3

- ☑ Romans 4-6
- ☑ Romans 7-9
- ☑ Romans 10-12
- ☑ Romans 13-16
- ☑ 1 Cor. 1-4
- ☑ 1 Cor. 5-9
- ☑ 1 Cor. 10-12
- ☑ 1 Cor. 13-16
- ☑ 2 Cor. 1-4
- ☑ 2 Cor. 5-8
- ☑ 2 Cor. 9-13
- ☑ Galatians 1-3
- ☑ Galatians 4-6
- ☑ Ephesians 1-3
- ☑ Ephesians 4-6
- ☑ Philippians 1-4
- ☑ Colossians 1-4
- ☑ 1 Thes. 1-3
- ☑ 1 Thes. 4-5
- ☑ 2 Thes. 1-3
- ☑ 1 Timothy 1-3
- ☑ 1 Timothy 4-6
- ☑ 2 Timothy 1-4
- ☑ Titus 1-3
- ☑ Philemon
- ☑ Hebrews 1
- ☑ Hebrews 2-4
- ☑ Hebrews 5-7
- ☑ Hebrews 8-10
- ☑ Hebrews 11-13
- ☑ James 1-3
- ☑ James 4-5
- ☐ 1 Peter 1-3
- ☐ 1 Peter 4-5
- ☐ 2 Peter 1-3
- ☐ 1 John 1-3
- ☐ 1 John 4-5
- ☐ 2 Jn, 3 Jn, Jude
- ☐ Revelation 1-3
- ☐ Revelation 4-6
- ☐ Revelation 7-9
- ☐ Rev. 10-12
- ☐ Rev. 13-15
- ☐ Rev. 16-18
- ☐ Rev. 19-22

Weeks 14-26

- ☐ Matthew 1-3
- ☐ Matthew 4-6
- ☐ Matthew 7-9
- ☐ Matt. 10-12
- ☐ Matt. 13-15
- ☐ Matt. 16-18
- ☐ Matt. 19-21
- ☐ Matt. 22-24
- ☐ Matt. 25-26
- ☐ Matt. 27-28
- ☐ Mark 1-3
- ☐ Mark 4-5
- ☐ Mark 6-8
- ☐ Mark 9-11
- ☐ Mark 12-14
- ☐ Mark 15-16
- ☐ Luke 1-2
- ☐ Luke 3-5
- ☐ Luke 6-7
- ☐ Luke 8-9
- ☐ Luke 10-11
- ☐ Luke 12-14
- ☐ Luke 15-17
- ☐ Luke 18-20
- ☐ Luke 21-22
- ☐ Luke 23-24
- ☐ John 1-3
- ☐ John 4-5
- ☐ John 6-7
- ☐ John 8-10
- ☐ John 11-12
- ☐ John 13-15
- ☐ John 16-18
- ☐ John 19-21
- ☐ Acts 1-3
- ☐ Acts 4-6
- ☐ Acts 7-8
- ☐ Acts 9-11
- ☐ Acts 12-15
- ☐ Acts 16-18
- ☐ Acts 19-21
- ☐ Acts 22-24
- ☐ Acts 25-26
- ☐ Acts 27-28
- ☐ Romans 1-3

- ☐ Romans 4-6
- ☐ Romans 7-9
- ☐ Romans 10-12
- ☐ Romans 13-16
- ☐ 1 Cor. 1-4
- ☐ 1 Cor. 5-9
- ☐ 1 Cor. 10-12
- ☐ 1 Cor. 13-16
- ☐ 2 Cor. 1-4
- ☐ 2 Cor. 5-8
- ☐ 2 Cor. 9-13
- ☐ Galatians 1-3
- ☐ Galatians 4-6
- ☐ Ephesians 1-3
- ☐ Ephesians 4-6
- ☐ Philippians 1-4
- ☐ Colossians 1-4
- ☐ 1 Thes. 1-3
- ☐ 1 Thes. 4-5
- ☐ 2 Thes. 1-3
- ☐ 1 Timothy 1-3
- ☐ 1 Timothy 4-6
- ☐ 2 Timothy 1-4
- ☐ Titus 1-3
- ☐ Philemon
- ☐ Hebrews 1
- ☐ Hebrews 2-4
- ☐ Hebrews 5-7
- ☐ Hebrews 8-10
- ☐ Hebrews 11-13
- ☐ James 1-3
- ☐ James 4-5
- ☐ 1 Peter 1-3
- ☐ 1 Peter 4-5
- ☐ 2 Peter 1-3
- ☐ 1 John 1-3
- ☐ 1 John 4-5
- ☐ 2 Jn, 3 Jn, Jude
- ☐ Revelation 1-3
- ☐ Revelation 4-6
- ☐ Revelation 7-9
- ☐ Rev. 10-12
- ☐ Rev. 13-15
- ☐ Rev. 16-18
- ☐ Rev. 19-22

Read through the new testament four times in one year

Weeks 27-39

- [ ] Matthew 1-3
- [ ] Matthew 4-6
- [ ] Matthew 7-9
- [ ] Matt. 10-12
- [ ] Matt. 13-15
- [ ] Matt. 16-18
- [ ] Matt. 19-21
- [ ] Matt. 22-24
- [ ] Matt. 25-26
- [ ] Matt. 27-28
- [ ] Mark 1-3
- [ ] Mark 4-5
- [ ] Mark 6-8
- [ ] Mark 9-11
- [ ] Mark 12-14
- [ ] Mark 15-16
- [ ] Luke 1-2
- [ ] Luke 3-5
- [ ] Luke 6-7
- [ ] Luke 8-9
- [ ] Luke 10-11
- [ ] Luke 12-14
- [ ] Luke 15-17
- [ ] Luke 18-20
- [ ] Luke 21-22
- [ ] Luke 23-24
- [ ] John 1-3
- [ ] John 4-5
- [ ] John 6-7
- [ ] John 8-10
- [ ] John 11-12
- [ ] John 13-15
- [ ] John 16-18
- [ ] John 19-21
- [ ] Acts 1-3
- [ ] Acts 4-6
- [ ] Acts 7-8
- [ ] Acts 9-11
- [ ] Acts 12-15
- [ ] Acts 16-18
- [ ] Acts 19-21
- [ ] Acts 22-24
- [ ] Acts 25-26
- [ ] Acts 27-28
- [ ] Romans 1-3

- [ ] Romans 4-6
- [ ] Romans 7-9
- [ ] Romans 10-12
- [ ] Romans 13-16
- [ ] 1 Cor. 1-4
- [ ] 1 Cor. 5-9
- [ ] 1 Cor. 10-12
- [ ] 1 Cor. 13-16
- [ ] 2 Cor. 1-4
- [ ] 2 Cor. 5-8
- [ ] 2 Cor. 9-13
- [ ] Galatians 1-3
- [ ] Galatians 4-6
- [ ] Ephesians 1-3
- [ ] Ephesians 4-6
- [ ] Phil. 1-4
- [ ] Colossians 1-4
- [ ] 1 Thes. 1-3
- [ ] 1 Thes. 4-5
- [ ] 2 Thes. 1-3
- [ ] 1 Timothy 1-3
- [ ] 1 Timothy 4-6
- [ ] 2 Timothy 1-4
- [ ] Titus 1-3
- [ ] Philemon
- [ ] Hebrews 1
- [ ] Hebrews 2-4
- [ ] Hebrews 5-7
- [ ] Hebrews 8-10
- [ ] Hebrews 11-13
- [ ] James 1-3
- [ ] James 4-5
- [ ] 1 Peter 1-3
- [ ] 1 Peter 4-5
- [ ] 2 Peter 1-3
- [ ] 1 John 1-3
- [ ] 1 John 4-5
- [ ] 2 Jn, 3 Jn, Jude
- [ ] Revelation 1-3
- [ ] Revelation 4-6
- [ ] Revelation 7-9
- [ ] Rev. 10-12
- [ ] Rev. 13-15
- [ ] Rev. 16-18
- [ ] Rev. 19-22

Weeks 40-52

- [ ] Matthew 1-3
- [ ] Matthew 4-6
- [ ] Matthew 7-9
- [ ] Matt. 10-12
- [ ] Matt. 13-15
- [ ] Matt. 16-18
- [ ] Matt. 19-21
- [ ] Matt. 22-24
- [ ] Matt. 25-26
- [ ] Matt. 27-28
- [ ] Mark 1-3
- [ ] Mark 4-5
- [ ] Mark 6-8
- [ ] Mark 9-11
- [ ] Mark 12-14
- [ ] Mark 15-16
- [ ] Luke 1-2
- [ ] Luke 3-5
- [ ] Luke 6-7
- [ ] Luke 8-9
- [ ] Luke 10-11
- [ ] Luke 12-14
- [ ] Luke 15-17
- [ ] Luke 18-20
- [ ] Luke 21-22
- [ ] Luke 23-24
- [ ] John 1-3
- [ ] John 4-5
- [ ] John 6-7
- [ ] John 8-10
- [ ] John 11-12
- [ ] John 13-15
- [ ] John 16-18
- [ ] John 19-21
- [ ] Acts 1-3
- [ ] Acts 4-6
- [ ] Acts 7-8
- [ ] Acts 9-11
- [ ] Acts 12-15
- [ ] Acts 16-18
- [ ] Acts 19-21
- [ ] Acts 22-24
- [ ] Acts 25-26
- [ ] Acts 27-28
- [ ] Romans 1-3

- [ ] Romans 4-6
- [ ] Romans 7-9
- [ ] Romans 10-12
- [ ] Romans 13-16
- [ ] 1 Cor. 1-4
- [ ] 1 Cor. 5-9
- [ ] 1 Cor. 10-12
- [ ] 1 Cor. 13-16
- [ ] 2 Cor. 1-4
- [ ] 2 Cor. 5-8
- [ ] 2 Cor. 9-13
- [ ] Galatians 1-3
- [ ] Galatians 4-6
- [ ] Ephesians 1-3
- [ ] Ephesians 4-6
- [ ] Phil. 1-4
- [ ] Colossians 1-4
- [ ] 1 Thes. 1-3
- [ ] 1 Thes. 4-5
- [ ] 2 Thes. 1-3
- [ ] 1 Timothy 1-3
- [ ] 1 Timothy 4-6
- [ ] 2 Timothy 1-4
- [ ] Titus 1-3
- [ ] Philemon
- [ ] Hebrews 1
- [ ] Hebrews 2-4
- [ ] Hebrews 5-7
- [ ] Hebrews 8-10
- [ ] Hebrews 11-13
- [ ] James 1-3
- [ ] James 4-5
- [ ] 1 Peter 1-3
- [ ] 1 Peter 4-5
- [ ] 2 Peter 1-3
- [ ] 1 John 1-3
- [ ] 1 John 4-5
- [ ] 2 Jn, 3 Jn, Jude
- [ ] Revelation 1-3
- [ ] Revelation 4-6
- [ ] Revelation 7-9
- [ ] Rev. 10-12
- [ ] Rev. 13-15
- [ ] Rev. 16-18
- [ ] Rev. 19-22

Bible reading schedule

Read through the Bible in one year! As you complete each daily reading, simply place a check in the appropriate box.

- ☐ 1 Genesis 1-3
- ☐ 2 Genesis 4:1-6:8
- ☐ 3 Genesis 6:9-9:29
- ☐ 4 Genesis 10-11
- ☐ 5 Genesis 12-14
- ☐ 6 Genesis 15-17
- ☐ 7 Genesis 18-19
- ☐ 8 Genesis 20-22
- ☐ 9 Genesis 23-24
- ☐ 10 Genesis 25-26
- ☐ 11 Genesis 27-28
- ☐ 12 Genesis 29-30
- ☐ 13 Genesis 31-32
- ☐ 14 Genesis 33-35
- ☐ 15 Genesis 36-37
- ☐ 16 Genesis 38-40
- ☐ 17 Genesis 41-42
- ☐ 18 Genesis 43-45
- ☐ 19 Genesis 46-47
- ☐ 20 Genesis 48-50
- ☐ 21 Job 1-3
- ☐ 22 Job 4-7
- ☐ 23 Job 8-11
- ☐ 24 Job 12-15
- ☐ 25 Job 16-19
- ☐ 26 Job 20-22
- ☐ 27 Job 23-28
- ☐ 28 Job 29-31
- ☐ 29 Job 32-34
- ☐ 30 Job 35-37
- ☐ 31 Job 38-42
- ☐ 32 Exodus 1-4
- ☐ 33 Exodus 5-8
- ☐ 34 Exodus 9-11
- ☐ 35 Exodus 12-13
- ☐ 36 Exodus 14-15
- ☐ 37 Exodus 16-18
- ☐ 38 Exodus 19-21
- ☐ 39 Exodus 22-24
- ☐ 40 Exodus 25-27
- ☐ 41 Exodus 28-29
- ☐ 42 Exodus 30-31
- ☐ 43 Exodus 32-34
- ☐ 44 Exodus 35-36
- ☐ 45 Exodus 37-38
- ☐ 46 Exodus 39-40
- ☐ 47 Leviticus 1:1-5:13
- ☐ 48 Leviticus 5:14-7:38
- ☐ 49 Leviticus 8-10
- ☐ 50 Leviticus 11-12
- ☐ 51 Leviticus 13-14
- ☐ 52 Leviticus 15-17
- ☐ 53 Leviticus 18-20
- ☐ 54 Leviticus 21-23
- ☐ 55 Leviticus 24-25
- ☐ 56 Leviticus 26-27
- ☐ 57 Numbers 1-2
- ☐ 58 Numbers 3-4
- ☐ 59 Numbers 5-6
- ☐ 60 Numbers 7
- ☐ 61 Numbers 8-10
- ☐ 62 Numbers 11-13
- ☐ 63 Numbers 14-15
- ☐ 64 Numbers 16-18
- ☐ 65 Numbers 19-21
- ☐ 66 Numbers 22-24
- ☐ 67 Numbers 25-26
- ☐ 68 Numbers 27-29
- ☐ 69 Numbers 30-31
- ☐ 70 Numbers 32-33
- ☐ 71 Numbers 34-36
- ☐ 72 Deuteronomy 1-2
- ☐ 73 Deuteronomy 3-4
- ☐ 74 Deuteronomy 5-7
- ☐ 75 Deuteronomy 8-10
- ☐ 76 Deuteronomy 11-13
- ☐ 77 Deuteronomy 14-17
- ☐ 78 Deuteronomy 18-21
- ☐ 79 Deuteronomy 22-25
- ☐ 80 Deuteronomy 26-28
- ☐ 81 Deuteronomy 29:1-31:29
- ☐ 82 Deuteronomy 31:30-34:12
- ☐ 83 Joshua 1-4
- ☐ 84 Joshua 5-8
- ☐ 85 Joshua 9-11
- ☐ 86 Joshua 12-14
- ☐ 87 Joshua 15-17
- ☐ 88 Joshua 18-19
- ☐ 89 Joshua 20-22
- ☐ 90 Joshua 23 - Judges 1
- ☐ 91 Judges 2-5
- ☐ 92 Judges 6-8
- ☐ 93 Judges 9
- ☐ 94 Judges 10-12
- ☐ 95 Judges 13-16
- ☐ 96 Judges 17-19
- ☐ 97 Judges 20-21
- ☐ 98 Ruth
- ☐ 99 1 Samuel 1-3
- ☐ 100 1 Samuel 4-7
- ☐ 101 1 Samuel 8-10
- ☐ 102 1 Samuel 11-13
- ☐ 103 1 Samuel 14-15
- ☐ 104 1 Samuel 16-17

Bible reading schedule

- ☐ 1 Genesis 1-3
- ☐ 2 Genesis 4:1-6:8
- ☐ 3 Genesis 6:9-9:29
- ☐ 4 Genesis 10-11
- ☐ 5 Genesis 12-14
- ☐ 6 Genesis 15-17
- ☐ 7 Genesis 18-19
- ☐ 8 Genesis 20-22
- ☐ 9 Genesis 23-24
- ☐ 10 Genesis 25-26
- ☐ 11 Genesis 27-28
- ☐ 12 Genesis 29-30
- ☐ 13 Genesis 31-32
- ☐ 14 Genesis 33-35
- ☐ 15 Genesis 36-37
- ☐ 16 Genesis 38-40
- ☐ 17 Genesis 41-42
- ☐ 18 Genesis 43-45
- ☐ 19 Genesis 46-47
- ☐ 20 Genesis 48-50
- ☐ 21 Job 1-3
- ☐ 22 Job 4-7
- ☐ 23 Job 8-11
- ☐ 24 Job 12-15
- ☐ 25 Job 16-19
- ☐ 26 Job 20-22
- ☐ 27 Job 23-28
- ☐ 28 Job 29-31
- ☐ 29 Job 32-34
- ☐ 30 Job 35-37
- ☐ 31 Job 38-42
- ☐ 32 Exodus 1-4
- ☐ 33 Exodus 5-8
- ☐ 34 Exodus 9-11
- ☐ 35 Exodus 12-13
- ☐ 36 Exodus 14-15
- ☐ 37 Exodus 16-18
- ☐ 38 Exodus 19-21
- ☐ 39 Exodus 22-24
- ☐ 40 Exodus 25-27
- ☐ 41 Exodus 28-29
- ☐ 42 Exodus 30-31
- ☐ 43 Exodus 32-34
- ☐ 44 Exodus 35-36
- ☐ 45 Exodus 37-38
- ☐ 46 Exodus 39-40
- ☐ 47 Leviticus 1:1-5:13
- ☐ 48 Leviticus 5:14-7:38
- ☐ 49 Leviticus 8-10
- ☐ 50 Leviticus 11-12
- ☐ 51 Leviticus 13-14
- ☐ 52 Leviticus 15-17
- ☐ 53 Leviticus 18-20
- ☐ 54 Leviticus 21-23
- ☐ 55 Leviticus 24-25
- ☐ 56 Leviticus 26-27
- ☐ 57 Numbers 1-2
- ☐ 58 Numbers 3-4
- ☐ 59 Numbers 5-6
- ☐ 60 Numbers 7
- ☐ 61 Numbers 8-10
- ☐ 62 Numbers 11-13
- ☐ 63 Numbers 14-15
- ☐ 64 Numbers 16-18
- ☐ 65 Numbers 19-21
- ☐ 66 Numbers 22-24
- ☐ 67 Numbers 25-26
- ☐ 68 Numbers 27-29
- ☐ 69 Numbers 30-31
- ☐ 70 Numbers 32-33
- ☐ 71 Numbers 34-36
- ☐ 72 Deuteronomy 1-2
- ☐ 73 Deuteronomy 3-4
- ☐ 74 Deuteronomy 5-7
- ☐ 75 Deuteronomy 8-10
- ☐ 76 Deuteronomy 11-13
- ☐ 77 Deuteronomy 14-17
- ☐ 78 Deuteronomy 18-21
- ☐ 79 Deuteronomy 22-25
- ☐ 80 Deuteronomy 26-28
- ☐ 81 Deuteronomy 29:1-31:29
- ☐ 82 Deuteronomy 31:30-34:12
- ☐ 83 Joshua 1-4
- ☐ 84 Joshua 5-8
- ☐ 85 Joshua 9-11
- ☐ 86 Joshua 12-14
- ☐ 87 Joshua 15-17
- ☐ 88 Joshua 18-19
- ☐ 89 Joshua 20-22
- ☐ 90 Joshua 23 - Judges 1
- ☐ 91 Judges 2-5
- ☐ 92 Judges 6-8
- ☐ 93 Judges 9
- ☐ 94 Judges 10-12
- ☐ 95 Judges 13-16
- ☐ 96 Judges 17-19
- ☐ 97 Judges 20-21
- ☐ 98 Ruth
- ☐ 99 1 Samuel 1-3
- ☐ 100 1 Samuel 4-7
- ☐ 101 1 Samuel 8-10
- ☐ 102 1 Samuel 11-13
- ☐ 103 1 Samuel 14-15
- ☐ 104 1 Samuel 16-17

Bible reading schedule
Day 200 - 288

- 200 2 Kings 19; 2 Chronicles 32:20-23; Isaiah 37
- 201 2 Kings 20; 2 Chronicles 32:24-33; Isaiah 38-39
- 202 2 Kings 21:1-18; 2 Chronicles 33:1-20; Isaiah 40
- 203 Isaiah 41-43
- 204 Isaiah 44-47
- 205 Isaiah 48-51
- 206 Isaiah 52-57
- 207 Isaiah 58-62
- 208 Isaiah 63-66
- 209 2 Kings 21:19-26; 2 Chronicles 33:21-34:7; Zephaniah
- 210 Jeremiah 1-3
- 211 Jeremiah 4-6
- 212 Jeremiah 7-9
- 213 Jeremiah 10-13
- 214 Jeremiah 14-16
- 215 Jeremiah 17-20
- 216 2 Kings 22:1-23:28; 2 Chronicles 34:8-35:19
- 217 Nahum; 2 Kings 23:29-37;
- 2 Chronicles 35:20-36:5; Jeremiah 22:10-17
- 218 Jeremiah 26; Habakkuk
- 219 Jeremiah 46-47; 2 Kings 24:1-4, 7; 2 Chronicles 36:6-7; Jeremiah 25, 35
- 220 Jeremiah 36, 45, 48
- 221 Jeremiah 49:1-33; Daniel 1-2
- 222 Jeremiah 22:18-30; 2 Kings 24:5-20; 2 Chronicles 36:8-12; Jeremiah 37:1-2; 52:1-3; 24; 29
- 223 Jeremiah 27-28, 23
- 224 Jeremiah 50-51
- 225 Jeremiah 49:34-39; 34:1-22; Ezekiel 1-3
- 226 Ezekiel 4-7
- 227 Ezekiel 8-11
- 228 Ezekiel 12-14
- 229 Ezekiel 15-17
- 230 Ezekiel 18-20
- 231 Ezekiel 21-23
- 232 2 Kings 25:1; 2 Chronicles 36:13-16; Jeremiah 39:1; 52:4; Ezekiel 24; Jeremiah 21:1-22:9; 32:1-44
- 233 Jeremiah 30-31, 33
- 234 Ezekiel 25; 29:1-16; 30; 31
- 235 Ezekiel 26-28
- 236 Jeremiah 37:3-39:10; 52:5-30; 2 Kings 25:2-21; 2 Chronicles 36:17-21
- 237 2 Kings 25:22; Jeremiah 39:11-40:6; Lamentations 1-3
- 238 Lamentations 4-5; Obadiah
- 239 Jeremiah 40:7-44:30; 2 Kings 25:23-26
- 240 Ezekiel 33:21-36:38
- 241 Ezekiel 37-39
- 242 Ezekiel 32:1-33:20; Daniel 3
- 243 Ezekiel 40-42
- 244 Ezekiel 43-45
- 245 Ezekiel 46-48
- 246 Ezekiel 29:17-21; Daniel 4; Jeremiah 52:31-34; 2 Kings 25:27-30; Psalm 44
- 247 Psalms 74; 79-80; 89
- 248 Psalms 85; 102; 106; 123; 137
- 249 Daniel 7-8; 5
- 250 Daniel 9; 6
- 251 2 Chronicles 36:22-23; Ezra 1:1-4:5
- 252 Daniel 10-12
- 253 Ezra 4:6-6:13; Haggai
- 254 Zechariah 1-6
- 255 Zechariah 7-8; Ezra 6:14-22; Psalm 78
- 256 Psalms 107; 116; 118
- 257 Psalms 125-26; 128-29; 132; 147; 149
- 258 Zechariah 9-14
- 259 Esther 1-4
- 260 Esther 5-10
- 261 Ezra 7-8
- 262 Ezra 9-10
- 263 Nehemiah 1-5
- 264 Nehemiah 6-7
- 265 Nehemiah 8-10
- 266 Nehemiah 11-13
- 267 Malachi
- 268 1 Chronicles 1-2
- 269 1 Chronicles 3-5
- 270 1 Chronicles 6
- 271 1 Chronicles 7:1-8:27
- 272 1 Chronicles 8:28-9:44
- 273 John 1:1-18; Mark 1:1; Luke 1:1-4; 3:23-38; Matthew 1:1-17
- 274 Luke 1:5-80
- 275 Matthew 1:18-2:23; Luke 2
- 276 Matthew 3:1-4:11; Mark 1:2-13; Luke 3:1-23; 4:1-13; John 1:19-34
- 277 John 1:35-3:36
- 278 John 4; Matthew 4:12-17; Mark 1:14-15; Luke 4:14-30
- 279 Mark 1:16-45; Matthew 4:18-25; 8:2-4, 14-17; Luke 4:31-5:16
- 280 Matthew 9:1-17; Mark 2:1-22; Luke 5:17-39
- 281 John 5; Matthew 12:1-21; Mark 2:23-3:12; Luke 6:1-11
- 282 Matthew 5; Mark 3:13-19; Luke 6:12-36
- 283 Matthew 6-7; Luke 6:37-49
- 284 Luke 7; Matthew 8:1, 5-13; 11:2-30
- 285 Matthew 12:22-50; Mark 3:20-35; Luke 8:1-21
- 286 Mark 4:1-34; Matthew 13:1-53
- 287 Mark 4:35-5:43; Matthew 8:18, 23-34; 9:18-34; Luke 8:22-56
- 288 Mark 6:1-30; Matthew 13:54-58; 9:35-11:1; 14:1-12; Luke 9:1-10

Bible reading schedule
Day 289 - 365

- [ ] 289 Matthew 14:13-36; Mark 6:31-56; Luke 9:11-17; John 6:1-21
- [ ] 290 John 6:22-7:1; Matthew 15:1-20; Mark 7:1-23
- [ ] 291 Matthew 15:21-16:20; Mark 7:24-8:30; Luke 9:18-21
- [ ] 292 Matthew 16:21-17:27; Mark 8:31-9:32; Luke 9:22-45
- [ ] 293 Matthew 18; 8:19-22; Mark 9:33-50; Luke 9:46-62; John 7:2-10
- [ ] 294 John 7:11-8:59
- [ ] 295 Luke 10:1-11:36
- [ ] 296 Luke 11:37-13:21
- [ ] 297 John 9-10
- [ ] 298 Luke 13:22-15:32
- [ ] 299 Luke 16:1-17:10; John 11:1-54
- [ ] 300 Luke 17:11-18:17; Matthew 19:1-15; Mark 10:1-16
- [ ] 301 Matthew 19:16-20:28; Mark 10:17-45; Luke 18:18-34
- [ ] 302 Matthew 20:29-34; 26:6-13; Mark 10:46-52; 14:3-9; Luke 18:35-19:28; John 11:55-12:11
- [ ] 303 Matthew 21:1-22; Mark 11:1-26; Luke 19:29-48; John 12:12-50
- [ ] 304 Matthew 21:23-22:14; Mark 11:27-12:12; Luke 20:1-19
- [ ] 305 Matthew 22:15-46; Mark 12:13-37; Luke 20:20-44
- [ ] 306 Matthew 23; Mark 12:38-44; Luke 20:45-21:4
- [ ] 307 Matthew 24:1-31; Mark 13:1-27; Luke 21:5-27
- [ ] 308 Matthew 24:32-26:5, 14-16; Mark 13:28-14:2, 10-11; Luke 21:28-22:6
- [ ] 309 Matthew 26:17-29; Mark 14:12-25; Luke 22:7-38; John 13
- [ ] 310 John 14-16
- [ ] 311 John 17:1-18:1; Matthew 26:30-46; Mark 14:26-42; Luke 22:39-46
- [ ] 312 Matthew 26:47-75; Mark 14:43-72; Luke 22:47-65; John 18:2-27
- [ ] 313 Matthew 27:1-26; Mark 15:1-15; Luke 22:66-23:25; John 18:28-19:16
- [ ] 314 Matthew 27:27-56; Mark 15:16-41; Luke 23:26-49; John 19:17-30
- [ ] 315 Matthew 27:57-28:8; Mark 15:42-16:8; Luke 23:50-24:12; John 19:31-20:10
- [ ] 316 Matthew 28:9-20; Mark 16:9-20; Luke 24:13-53; John 20:11-21:25
- [ ] 317 Acts 1-2
- [ ] 318 Acts 3-5
- [ ] 319 Acts 6:1-8:1
- [ ] 320 Acts 8:2-9:43
- [ ] 321 Acts 10-11
- [ ] 322 Acts 12-13
- [ ] 323 Acts 14-15
- [ ] 324 Galatians 1-3
- [ ] 325 Galatians 4-6
- [ ] 326 James
- [ ] 327 Acts 16:1-18:11
- [ ] 328 1 Thessalonians
- [ ] 329 2 Thessalonians; Acts 18:12-19:22
- [ ] 330 1 Corinthians 1-4
- [ ] 331 1 Corinthians 5-8
- [ ] 332 1 Corinthians 9-11
- [ ] 333 1 Corinthians 12-14
- [ ] 334 1 Corinthians 15-16
- [ ] 335 Acts 19:23-20:1; 2 Corinthians 1-4
- [ ] 336 2 Corinthians 5-9
- [ ] 337 2 Corinthians 10-13
- [ ] 338 Romans 1-3
- [ ] 339 Romans 4-6
- [ ] 340 Romans 7-8
- [ ] 341 Romans 9-11
- [ ] 342 Romans 12-15
- [ ] 343 Romans 16; Acts 20:2-21:16
- [ ] 344 Acts 21:17-23:35
- [ ] 345 Acts 24-26
- [ ] 346 Acts 27-28
- [ ] 347 Ephesians 1-3
- [ ] 348 Ephesians 4-6
- [ ] 349 Colossians
- [ ] 350 Philippians
- [ ] 351 Philemon; 1 Timothy 1-3
- [ ] 352 1 Timothy 4-6; Titus
- [ ] 353 2 Timothy
- [ ] 354 1 Peter
- [ ] 355 Jude; 2 Peter
- [ ] 356 Hebrews 1:1-5:10
- [ ] 357 Hebrews 5:11-9:28
- [ ] 358 Hebrews 10-11
- [ ] 359 Hebrews 12-13; 2 John; 3 John
- [ ] 360 1 John
- [ ] 361 Revelation 1-3
- [ ] 362 Revelation 4-9
- [ ] 363 Revelation 10-14
- [ ] 364 Revelation 15-18
- [ ] 365 Revelation 19-22

From the Liberty Bible, King James Version. Copyright ©1975, Thomas Nelson, Inc. Publishers. Used by permission.

QuietTime

WEEK 1

When you sin, God doesn't say "Oops!" When those you call friends turn against you, God doesn't say "See ya!" This week we will see that God is faithful even when we aren't; even when we're abandoned by those we thought we could trust.

Prayer focus for this week

THE QUESTION · *What is the writer saying?*
THE ANSWER · *How Can I apply this to my life?*

Sunday · PSALM 51:1-19

Q

A

DIGGING DEEPER · David writes these words as he struggles with the reality of his sin of adultery and murder. He went from being confronted by Nathan the Prophet (2 Samuel 12:7-9) to the realization that he had sinned against a holy God. David knew God had used Nathan to bring the truth and that God was pursuing discipline in his life. David pleaded three things: mercy, which only God can grant; cleansing, which only God can do; and restoration, which only God can approve. God will not allow sin to reign in the hearts of His children. Just as He loved David enough to confront the truth of his sin, God will do the same for you, His child.

How does God reveal sin in your life? Is He able to use the regular reading of His Word or must He send messengers? Are there areas in your life that are "undone" before God?

Monday · PSALM 52:1-9

Q

A

DIGGING DEEPER • David boldly declares God's promise of judgment against those who come against His people. He has come to understand the reality that oftentimes the wicked will seem to be powerful, growing in wealth, and even appear to be "blessed" by their pursuits. But there will be a day when those who love God will receive their inheritance and the wicked will receive their judgment. David refers to himself as an "olive tree." Olive trees symbolize fruitful, abundant life...as God is rich in mercy and love. David trusts God in all things because of this: he knows the Lord will take care not only of his enemies, but of his life as well.
Do you ever look at your lost friends and think that their lives appear to be more fun than yours? How can you relate these verses with your struggles to remain faithful to the Lord?

Tuesday · PSALM 53:1-6

Q

A

DIGGING DEEPER • It is a foolish thing to say there is no God. These verses do not mean that people are not intelligent enough to comprehend God's existence. They proclaim that those who do not take seriously God's sovereign existence are fools! In other words, there is no excuse for one who denies God. In Romans 1:18-20, the Apostle Paul declares that creation itself is enough evidence to prove God's existence, leaving no excuse for anyone to deny Him. Also, as children of God, we are to be careful not to make light of God's name in any way.
What is your response to those in your school who say there is no God? Are you making light of God's name in any way that would cause your friends not to take God seriously?

Wednesday · PSALM 54:1-7

Q

A

DIGGING DEEPER • David is making an urgent plea for protection against the armies of King Saul. Remember, King Saul loved David at first, but because David was favored by Israel, Saul turned against him (1 Samuel 23:19-29). Saul grew cold towards God and was jealous of David's accomplishments. This type of battle was very hard because it involved one who was once a friend. But David relied upon God for deliverance and defense against Saul and his attacks. For us, too, the toughest battles are sometimes experienced with those who were once close to us, but have turned against us because of our walk with Christ.

Do you have friends that have turned against you because you drew closer to God? Were some of these friends once excited about God? How can you deal with the attacks of these "friends"?

Thursday · PSALM 55:1-14

Q

A

DIGGING DEEPER • At times, life gets to the point where we want to run away to the farthest place to get away from a tough situation. In today's reading, David wanted to run from those who had turned against him. He was disappointed that his close friends turned against him, and he feared their power. But then David realized that God was greater and more powerful than their evil. David acted in faith by asking God to confuse the wicked (v. 9) and be his refuge.

Do you ever get to the place where you feel like running away from a hard situation? Most of us rarely receive persecution for our faith, but we do sometimes want to run from situations that are caused by our sin. Maybe it's time to run to God instead of running to our sin!

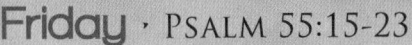

Friday · PSALM 55:15-23

Q

A

DIGGING DEEPER • These verses show that David has settled down and has begun to remember the promises of God to those who love Him and live for Him. David finally casts his cares upon God (v. 22) and understands that his Lord will punish the ungodly in His own timing. David resolves in the end to trust only in God—not to rely on what he could do for himself, or worry about what the ungodly could do to him, but only to trust in his Lord.

When was the last time you simply trusted God? Are you in a place where you know the walls are starting to crash in on your life? It's in times like these when you need to lay down your life on the foundation of Christ...simple faith in the knowledge that God loves you. Do it now!

Saturday · PSALM 56:1-13

Q

A

DIGGING DEEPER • What can mortal man do to me? What a great question for a child of God to consider. As David experienced the pain of close friends and family turning against him, Christ has promised that you will experience that, too. Jesus said that He did not come to bring peace, but a sword; and your own household will come against you (Matthew 10:34-36). It is hard to find comfort in that promise, but as much as you have received Christ, those close to you might reject Him even more.

Ask God to give you boldness today. Ask Him to grant you a willing spirit to be faithful to the end. Remember, suffering is as much a part of living for Christ as enjoying summer camp is!

QuietTime

WEEK 2

When you were a kid, did you ever build a fort or hideout? As much as we wanted to make that thing strong, it usually fell apart pretty easily. This week we will find out that God is a mighty fortress, unchanged by the storms of life. He is a refuge for those who seek Him. Check it out!

Prayer focus for this week

THE QUESTION   *What is the writer saying?*
THE ANSWER   *How Can I apply this to my life?*

Sunday · PSALM 57:1-11

Q
A

DIGGING DEEPER · Sometimes it seems like we are a lot more ready to move forward than God is! In today's verses, David is asking God to catch up with him. He is saying, "God, my heart is ready for You to move. I'll even sing You the songs You love to hear." One of the hardest parts of the Christian walk is waiting on God to deliver what He has promised. Whether judging the wicked, answering our prayers, fulfilling our heart's desires, or giving a blessing…we must remember that God is never too late or too early. He is always right on time!

Do you truly trust God's sovereignty? Are you willing to be patient and wait on the Lord to do His work in your life and in the lives of those around you? Are you working for God or fighting against Him with your impatience?

Monday · Psalm 58:1-11

Q

A

DIGGING DEEPER • There are times when God allows wicked leadership to reign over His people. Most of the time God uses this as an act of chastening to cause us to repent and draw closer to Him. Our country has experienced this in the past, when lies were told and cover-ups were made. At the same time, this leadership acted as our judge and gave direction. But according to this Psalm of David, God will judge them and He will protect and reward those who are His, even in the darkest of times.

When you see the word "reward" as a promise from God to those who love Him, what do you think it means? When you hear the words "peace" and "joy," what do they mean for the believer even in the toughest of times?

Tuesday · Psalm 59:1-17

Q

A

DIGGING DEEPER • When David talks about God being his "fortress" it is very significant, because it means that God is the ultimate refuge and protection from a pursuing enemy for the kingdom over which He reigns. A fortress is always built in a strategic location on higher ground, so the enemy cannot make a surprise attack that could go unseen. A fortress is built to withstand the pounding of firepower and house the innocent during attacks. According to David, God is his fortress and refuge in times of trouble.

Where do you place your trust today? When you are hit hard by temptation and accusations from the enemy, do you run to God as your refuge? Thank God for His pure love and strength today. Run to Him!

Wednesday · PSALM 60:1-12

DIGGING DEEPER • These verses may sound like God has forsaken David and his land, but if you look closely, you will see that David is proclaiming God's sovereign control over all things. David's not blaming God; he's recognizing the rule and authority of God over all men and things. David knows that Israel has forsaken God and that the people have caused God to withdraw His blessings. But at the same time, he is calling to God for restoration and help, knowing that God is the only one who can give it.

As a Christian, imagine fighting a war without the hand of God behind your army. Has God had to withdraw His blessings on your life because you have forsaken His commands? There is nothing more pitiful than a child of God who is powerless because of sin!

Thursday · PSALM 61:1-8

DIGGING DEEPER • King David has become weary from the battles against those who were once close and now have turned against him. He is worn out from leading an army that is powerless because of their rebellion against God. As he writes these verses, he remembers the days when it seemed like God was huge and very near. His prayers were powerful and real…God could do anything! It's like remembering Christian summer camp a few years back where God rocked your world, but now He seems a million miles away. Why and how did this happen?

Do you long to dwell in God's tent forever? Is God your refuge and shelter? Or, have the things of this world choked you? Consider what it means to draw near to God. Are you willing to draw near to Him today?

Friday · PSALM 62:1-12

DIGGING DEEPER · In these verses, David has found rest in the Lord even in the midst of difficult times. But even though he has turned to God and found rest, that doesn't mean the trouble is gone. David is resting in the Lord now, which means that he has given all his struggles and trials to God, knowing that He will give him wisdom and strength to get through them. Notice that David has not asked for the trials to go away, but that he is seeking God for the power to work through them. A huge turning point in your life as a believer is when you ask God to find you faithful through trials rather than asking Him to get you out of them! David finally claimed that God is strong and that He WILL reward us according to what we have done.

How do you pray through trials? Do you pray for strength, or for a ripcord to get out? Select an area in your life that you will entrust to Him today.

Saturday · PSALM 63:1-11

DIGGING DEEPER · Has there been a day when you came to realize that you were a sinner and needed a Savior? If so, remember what it was like? You thirsted for God. Your soul desired to be consumed by the forgiving power of God. You wanted God to make your life new. You were desperate for God to change your life. In John 4:10-14, Christ referred to Himself as "living water." In today's reading, David claims his thirst for God and proclaims that God alone satisfies his soul.

Is God's love better than life itself? Are you truly thirsty for the presence of God? Are you earnestly seeking Him? What makes you thirsty for God... the desert of material things of this world? Or, do you simply desire more of Him everyday just because God is good?

QuietTime

WEEK 3

How HUGE is God to you? This week we will see it all. God is sovereign over life, death, friends, created things, and our lives. It's all about resting in His incredible "God-sized" hand and allowing Him to be the Father you might never have had.

Prayer focus for this week

THE QUESTION · *What is the writer saying?*
THE ANSWER · *How Can I apply this to my life?*

Sunday · PSALM 64:1-10

DIGGING DEEPER • David uses a very real word when describing people that are trying to ruin his life: "insurrection," which means "to conspire against or revolt." David has asked God to hide him from the revolt of the wicked who are against those who love the Lord. He wants nothing to do with the way they think or work. His life is contrary to all they consider life to be. David sees that their plan and desire is to take down the innocent with them. Knowing the power of sin, David has called on God to deal with them. There are friends in your life that are clearly in revolt against God. But there are also friends that are sensitive and open to hear about God.
Inventory those you call friends. Where do they line up with regard to your life as a believer? Do not make life-long friendships or go places where the Spirit of God is not at work!

Monday · PSALM 65:1-13

Q

A

DIGGING DEEPER •   It is an incredible thing to be a child of God! David has just listed his praises to God because he is moved and grateful for God's forgiveness. Understanding God's forgiveness is a key to praise and worship. Praise comes from gratitude, and gratitude comes from the realization that God paid in full our debt of sin. David praised God because He "purged" or "forgave" his sin. Notice the past tense of those words. It should be on our hearts always to praise God for sending His Son, Jesus Christ as the atonement for our sin. It would be a shame for anyone who calls himself a Christian to get over the fact that Christ died for us, and that, therefore, God forgave our sins.

Is the message of the cross still fresh in your life? Maybe you're not living it because you're not sharing it! Share Christ today...at all costs!

Tuesday · PSALM 66:1-20

Q

A

DIGGING DEEPER •   This is an AWESOME Psalm! David tells the whole story of how God rules over everything. He tells how God uses distress in our lives to refine us and make us call on Him for deliverance and hope. There is nothing more powerful in a believer's life than when God proves and tries (vv. 10-11) our hearts. It may hurt but it causes purification and growth. You can be certain that God does not listen to you if you hide sin in your heart. However, God wants you to know that He is listening if you are living under His laws and promises.

Can you say, "Blessed be God, which hath not turned away prayer"? Are you regarding hidden sin in your life? Why is it so important to allow God to deal with sin every day?

Wednesday · PSALM 67:1-7

Q
A

DIGGING DEEPER • Most people think eternal life is just about Heaven. In John 10:10, when Jesus talked about life in Him, He used the word "abundantly." Jesus wasn't just talking about abundance in Heaven; He was talking about it here, too. This Psalm tells of the abundance God has given, and that He will give it here on earth to those who love Him and praise His name. Abundant life isn't about material things, and the blessings of God aren't always physical, either. But God promises a harvest of blessings to those who praise His name at all times. This Psalm helps to remind us that God is the God of Heaven AND earth.
When was the last time you sat down and considered the blessings of God in your life? Maybe God is due a praise report from you today!

Thursday · PSALM 68:1-10

Q
A

DIGGING DEEPER • Most students don't understand the "fatherhood" of God. Most of us think that God is waiting to hurl lightening bolts and thunder at us when we mess up. But that's not true! In verse 5, it says that God is a "father to the fatherless." Also, in verse 6, He says He will set the solitary or the lonely in "families." This means God will never leave us alone as orphans. Even if your own earthly father leaves you, God will provide a father figure in your life. This proves that God does not seek to set you loose. He's not waiting for you to make a mistake and punish you. God is a provider! Sometimes that provision is discipline, but as a father He will provide us with all we need.
Do you see God in the same way you see your earthly father? Are you allowing Him to be your provider for everything?

Friday · Psalm 68:11-23

Q

A

DIGGING DEEPER • Funerals are huge alarm clocks! People tend to get real focused on life when they experience the death of someone close to them. Not too many students woke up today worrying or even thinking about death. It's mostly because you think you have your whole life left to live. That's probably true for most students, but death is an absolute! Hebrews 9:27 claims that all of us have an appointment with death at some specific time. In today's Psalm, David claims an incredible truth in verse 20, which says, "...unto God belong the issues from death." This verse claims God to be the ruler over and the power to overcome death-not to keep death from happening, but to take away its cost and penalty.
There is a difference between not thinking about death and not worrying about death...which one applies to you?

Saturday · Psalm 68:24-35

Q

A

DIGGING DEEPER • If there was a parade for God, who would take part in it? Who would be leading the procession? In today's reading, David draws a picture of that parade. Verses 24-28 tell of a victorious procession to the sanctuary that David had prepared for worship before Solomon's temple was built. You would think that no one would be worthy to walk before the Lord, but according to these verses the congregation of believers will be His parade. Israel is God's fountain, and today we can join His congregation by accepting Christ and becoming a part of that spiritual procession. We can only come into His courts and bring God the praise that He is due because of the righteousness of Christ, and by trusting Him.
Can you be in God's parade? Have you received the righteousness of Christ? Imagine all believers together in one place praising God!

QuietTime

WEEK 4

What would life be like if it was like summer camp all the time? Christianity isn't just about mountaintop experiences; it includes valleys and climbs too! This week is about trusting God at all times. Plug in and stay on it all this week and see what happens!

Prayer focus for this week

THE QUESTION *What is the writer saying?*
THE ANSWER *How Can I apply this to my life?*

Sunday · PSALM 69:1-12

DIGGING DEEPER • Trusting God in everything is not an easy task. It is a walk that begins the day we accept Christ as our personal Savior. Trusting God with eternity is one thing, but trusting Him with the "now stuff" is another. The hard parts are when we have to wait, are caught in our sin, or are enduring hardship. When it seems like God isn't answering our prayers immediately, or the way we want Him to, we just jump in and take control so it will all come in our timing. Or, just in case God doesn't come through, we take it over in our own power. This Psalm expresses these times when we want to be faithful and we know that God is always faithful...but we get tired and find ourselves wishing for something good to happen.

In what areas of life do you have a hard time trusting God? Why do you think God's timing is, at times, much different than yours?

Monday · PSALM 69:13-21

Q

A

DIGGING DEEPER • Imagine what it would be like to have no hope at all. Consider the thought of not having a relationship with Jesus Christ. It's amazing how easy it is to forget what it was like to be lost and apart from God's gift of salvation. As a child of God, even the deepest and darkest days are full of hope because of God's love for His children. God is faithful even when we are not! God IS faithful because it is His character to deliver what He has promised…God has never been wrong. Today's reading shows that David is at the edge of total loss, but he knows he won't go down, only because God is faithful.

What would it be like to be lost again? What is it that makes you need God the most? When does God hear from you? Is it during exam time and in tough trials? Maybe that's why your life is always a test or a crisis!

Tuesday · PSALM 69:22-36

Q

A

DIGGING DEEPER • If you were shopping for a Christmas gift for God, what do you think you would get Him? Imagine trying to get something for someone that already has everything! Many of us think that God has this list of things He wants and that we are supposed to try and fill His shopping list. According to today's Psalm, in vv. 30-31, David has come to understand that God is not looking for something—He just wants us. God seeks the praise of His people. God seeks to be glorified through your life. All God wants is your praise, worship, and a surrendered life.

What do you think God considers a worthy offering from you today? Have you surrendered your life to God? What could you praise Him for today?

Wednesday · Psalm 70:1-5

DIGGING DEEPER • Have you ever heard of a "Hail Mary" pass in football? The team is desperate and there is only one chance left: pass or fail. This Psalm brings out the reality of readiness and trust that we need to have in the toughest of times. Many of us send God "Hail Mary" prayers as a last ditch effort to try and win, with a final prayer of desperation just in case God is listening. Our daily walk should be full of prayers and petitions to God, not just when the going is tough. Knowing God intimately is a great key to remember when your back is up against the wall. **One question today...is talking to God a habit for you, or a "Hail Mary" pass? Maybe you should spend some time with Him today, thanking Him for all that He has done. You can begin by thanking Him for your salvation.**

Thursday · Psalm 71:1-13

DIGGING DEEPER • What would it be like if God got tired of saving people? What would happen if God got sick and tired of rescuing you from troubles and trials? Today's Scripture reveals that it is God's nature and character to save AND to rescue, or help us to escape disaster. Being a Christian does not promise an easy life full of campfire songs and eating "S'mores." But being a Christian promises hope and certainty that God will save and deliver His children. It doesn't necessarily mean that we will live to a ripe old age, but it does mean that even in our death, we will not be separated from the love and presence of God. God NEVER gets tired of saving people, nor will He ever forsake rescuing you...even from yourself! **When was the last time God used your testimony to reveal His saving power? Reveal God at school today with a personal word of testimony!**

Friday · PSALM 71:14-24

Q

A

DIGGING DEEPER • Have you heard the statement, "Share your faith in Christ at all times, and if necessary, use words"? This sounds good, but it's not biblical! Yeah, it's important to live your life as an example, but most people use that as a cop out for not sharing their faith through words, too. Not too many people will walk up to you and say, "Hey, I see by the way you act that you're a Christian. Can I have that?" They will see a difference, but you MUST tell people why. This Psalm has "telling people about God" all over it. We are called to use our mouths to proclaim God's righteousness and mighty acts and to declare God's power to the next generation…all day, every day.
Is your life an example of God's power? Is your mouth proclaiming what you believe? For the cause of Christ, words are as important as action!

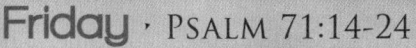

Saturday · PSALM 72:1-11

Q

A

DIGGING DEEPER • If you were President, how would you run our country? You would probably want to change a lot of the bad things that were brought in by past administrations. You would want to see our country restored to a godly nation, allowing open prayer and Biblical teaching in schools. Those are all good, but what about you personally? What kind of character do you have when no one else is around? In these verses, we see that the character of a nation is based on the character of its leadership. We are commanded to pray for those in positions of leadership. Remember that the only truly perfect government will be when Christ rules here on earth during the millennial kingdom, as this Psalm promises.
Are you the same alone as you are in public? How are you leading people around you? Are you praying for our President as he has asked?

QuietTime

WEEK 5

Why do lost people have all the fun? What was God thinking when He allowed this? Hello, is anyone home in Heaven? It's tough down here! This week look at what God says about His faithfulness to those who remain faithful to Him.

Prayer focus for this week

THE QUESTION *What is the writer saying?*
THE ANSWER *How Can I apply this to my life?*

Sunday · PSALM 72:12-20

Q

A

DIGGING DEEPER · If Christ ran for President, would He win? When you listen to what people want, it all sounds good. World peace, no poverty, no crime, everyone will have a job, etc. What would Christ promise the people if He were elected? Do you think world peace fits into what Christ has set out to accomplish? These verses reveal the character of the nation and people that have Christ as their King. There will still be enemies, but they will not prevail against a nation that is led by God, because He will be their defense. Christ will be king here on earth one day, and bring about all that this Psalm describes.

How can you help draw our country back to a nation under God's power? How will you impact those around you this week as you serve God?

Monday · PSALM 73:1-14

Q

A

DIGGING DEEPER • When being witnessed to, a geology student responded by saying, "No way! Why would I want to do that? I have everything I need...I'm having the time of my life." How come lost people have all the fun? Shouldn't a child of God have a better life than those apart from Christ have? These are questions you have probably wanted to ask God a time or two. The writer of this Psalm is petitioning these very questions to God. At times it seems defeating to watch the world laugh and party while you hammer out your faith in Christ. But remember, this world is not ours. We are strangers because of our promised inheritance in eternity. Sometimes it's hard to think that far ahead, but it will be worth the wait.
How long is a party? How long is eternity? Isn't what God has in store worth the wait?

Tuesday · PSALM 73:15-28

Q

A

DIGGING DEEPER • Wow! The writer found the answers to his question from yesterday. The times when you feel like you're missing out on "life" by being a Christian come when your focus is not on God. Verse 17 tells us that Christianity became cool again when "... I went into the sanctuary of God; then understood I their end." As soon as you meet with God, His love and presence will remind you of the hope that there is in Christ. Remember, suffering and struggling is as much a part of the Gospel as forgiveness and Heaven. You would be surprised at how many "party-ers" wish they had the life you have.
What price was paid for your life in Christ? Grow your passion to reach those who "party" rather than seeking their sin.

Wednesday · PSALM 74:1-12

DIGGING DEEPER · Can God bless America? This slogan is everywhere now, but…CAN God bless America? Why should He? This Psalm is a cry for help from the nation of Israel who has been defeated. Their enemy desolates the sanctuary of God. The psalmist feels as though God has left His people. Regardless of what God will do with us as a nation, the key is to remain faithful and be busy at work for the cause of Christ. This is the time for those who love Him to continually claim and serve Him as their King (v. 12). No matter how rough it gets, God will remain faithful to those who are faithful to Him.

Are you living as you ought to be living in light of Christ's return? How important is God to you these days?

Thursday · PSALM 74:13-23

DIGGING DEEPER · Have you ever been in a situation where you felt like you needed to remind God what He promised those who love Him? Usually, in the end, you receive comfort in just thinking about all He is doing, has done, and will do. The situation doesn't go away, but the fear does. In today's Psalm, the writer lists God's promises and mighty works, not so much for God as for his own understanding that God will deliver everything He promised in His sovereign time. It's still a plea, but that plea is full of hope because God is faithful. Rest assured there is a purpose for all things, with the result being that God gets the glory.

Have you ever reminded God of the promises He has given to those who love Him? If not, is it because you don't know His promises? Why is there such comfort in knowing God's promises?

Friday · PSALM 75:1-10

DIGGING DEEPER • Being a judge would be pretty cool—deciding who was right and who was wrong and then sentencing them according to what you felt they deserved. How about lost people, too...haven't you wanted to go ahead and tell them what they will get because of their actions? Be honest with yourself. It is a temptation to be the judge from time to time. These verses remind us that God is the Judge, and He will rule with perfect righteousness. Though you are not called to be the judge of others, you have a responsibility to uphold and declare God's laws and covenants. We ARE called to judge ourselves (1 Corinthians 11:31) so that we are sober about our sin and humbled through God's forgiveness.
Are you guilty of judging others? Could that be from a lack of love for others? Have you thanked God for His great forgiveness lately?

Saturday · PSALM 76:1-12

DIGGING DEEPER • How powerful is God? It is easy at times to think God is like an empty light bulb socket. We think that when we sin and forsake His holiness, He'll just stick our finger in the socket and give us a little shock. Maybe it's time to consider the fact that God created everything by His own hand...not with power tools! Though it is not God's goal to hurl lightening bolts at people, He is still holy and worthy to be obeyed. The earth and stars obey God, yet for some reason, man thinks he can do what he wants, whenever he wants. Today we are reminded that by God's hand, all things are held together and move as He commands, and He will judge all things perfectly.
When was the last time you even considered God's majesty? How holy is God to you? Is your life proof of His holiness?

QuietTime

WEEK 6

1 Timothy is awesome! It's like a letter to a good buddy. A young pastor needs some instruction on how to handle some problems at his church. His best friend writes him and gives him help. Funny thing is, the problems are the same things we struggle with. God has something just for you this week!

Prayer focus for this week

THE QUESTION — *What is the writer saying?*
THE ANSWER — *How Can I apply this to my life?*

Sunday · 1 TIMOTHY 1:1-11

Q

A

DIGGING DEEPER · Timothy was a young pastor in a city called Ephesus. Paul was the guy who helped Timothy grow as a Christian for many years. Paul was writing to help Timothy handle some problems in the church. The big problem was that people in the church were not teaching God's Word correctly. In fact, they were stirring up some trouble and arguments. You'd think Timothy could handle it himself since he was the pastor, right? All of us can use help in our Christian walk. Everyone needs a *Paul* in his life—an older Christian who can help us grow and live like God wants us to.

Who is your Paul in your Christian walk? Do you have a great desire to learn from him? If you don't have someone, would you be willing to find someone to help you grow?

Monday · 1 TIMOTHY 1:12-20

Q

A

DIGGING DEEPER • Don't you wish you knew where there was some buried treasure? Actually, if you know Christ, you already possess the greatest treasure in the world. If you don't feel like that, it's simply because you need to be as grateful and thankful for your salvation as Paul was. Paul knew he was a sinner, and that somehow, although he didn't deserve it, Christ pardoned all his sin. How precious to you is your salvation? Yes, we're glad we're saved, but are we thankful enough to be unquestionably faithful to our Lord? If you measure your thankfulness by your commitment to the Lord, how thankful are you, really? We could all be more thankful! **Would you commit to thanking the Lord for your salvation throughout the day? Can people see your thankfulness in your dedication to the Lord?**

Tuesday · 1 TIMOTHY 2:1-8

Q

A

DIGGING DEEPER • Paul is giving some instruction on how prayer should work in the church. We ought to ask for the needs of others, worship the Lord, and also express thankfulness. The key element in prayer is understanding that Christ made it possible to pray. No one comes to the Father except through Christ. That's why we often pray "...in Jesus' Name." Jesus also died for all people. There were some enemies in this church. The people were to pray for everyone, even people with whom they were having problems. We also need to be ready to pray for those with whom we have problems. If Christ died for all people we must pray for all people. **With whom are you having a conflict right now? Are you praying for the Lord to help him, and to help you resolve it? Whom can you add to your prayer list who does not know Christ?**

Wednesday · 1 TIMOTHY 2:9-15

DIGGING DEEPER • Apparently there were some ladies causing problems in the church. These women were concerned about the way they looked on the outside. Paul said they should be dressed up with "good works." The inside is what counts! The other inward problem these women struggled with was humility. Both men and women need to be submissive and humble. Even Christ was submissive to the Father's will. These women were more concerned about causing trouble than about learning. Learning is one of the main reasons we all go to church. The goal is not to show how smart we are, but to learn from God's Word. It's hard to learn if we're the ones doing all the talking!

Are you more concerned about your outward appearance than your heart attitude toward God? Are you the kind of person who's eager to learn?

Thursday · 1 TIMOTHY 3:1-7

DIGGING DEEPER • Are you the kind of person who likes to be in charge? Be careful—leadership is not easy! There were people in Timothy's church that wanted to be pastors. That's good, but there are some requirements for being a pastor. One of the biggest ones is to be "blameless." They needed to be the people you couldn't point the finger at and accuse of living wrongly. That means they needed to be very spiritually mature, and not new to the Christian walk. How could they help someone else grow if they hadn't first been growing for many years? Leadership is about being the right person, not being in the right position.

Is being in charge more important to you than being a godly person? What should you change in order to be a godly leader someday?

Friday · 1 TIMOTHY 3:8-16

DIGGING DEEPER •   Yesterday we looked at what a pastor ought to be. Today we're looking at another position in the church: deacon. The key word to remember about a deacon is *servant*. These are people who are to be directly under the pastor, but who do whatever is necessary to serve the church. These people are critical for the church today. They don't necessarily have authority, but they serve the Lord and serve others. There's no job too low for them. They'll do whatever it takes to serve others. This may sound like a dirty job, but it is a great honor to serve in a local church. Maybe we're not all deacons, but we all should be willing to serve others.
Would you be willing to pick two ways you can serve someone today? Are you willing to do any job that will help others?

Saturday · 1 TIMOTHY 4:1-8

DIGGING DEEPER • Ever watch the Olympics? Olympians are chiseled athletes who perform at the highest level. They only compete every four years. So what do people do for four years while they wait? TRAIN! They work out and get ready. The same things should be true of Christians, except our Olympics are every day! We discipline ourselves to live godly lives. We train the inside—like our heart and our mind—ourselves just our body. That's just the opposite of what some people were doing at Timothy's church. They were teaching lies and training people to follow ungodly rules instead of following Christ. *Our* training schedule includes things like quiet time, Scripture memory, church attendance, prayer, and learning God's Word!
Are you giving the Lord a half-hearted effort in your Christian training? Have you been training yourself to be ungodly?

QuietTime

WEEK 7

Life would be really fun if it weren't for people, right? Parents, teachers, bosses, and everybody else mess up our fun, huh? Timothy had tough people to deal with, too. You'll see it this week, and we'll end with a big-time issue: MONEY! How do you handle it, and what do you do with it? Check it out! You might be surprised!

Prayer focus for this week

THE QUESTION · *What is the writer saying?*
THE ANSWER · *How Can I apply this to my life?*

Sunday · 1 TIMOTHY 4:9-16

DIGGING DEEPER · "People don't trust me!" "Nobody believes I can make a difference!" Ever think thoughts like this? Timothy might have. If Timothy was to get anything from this letter, this is what Paul wanted him to remember! This is Paul's main focus for Timothy! The message is basically this: Just keep doing what a pastor is supposed to be doing! Even if people look down on you, just keep teaching the Word. Set the right example for everyone (v. 12). Make sure you believe and teach exactly what God says. People can criticize us, but if we are being faithful to God in all aspects of our lives, their words have little effect. Our job is to be faithful to God's Word and God's work. That is our focus!

Is there any area of your life in which you're not being faithful? Are you focusing on your critics or on pleasing God?

Monday · 1 TIMOTHY 5:1-8

Q

A

DIGGING DEEPER • Because some of Timothy's critics were older men, Paul gave him some instruction on how to be respectful to them, while still correcting biblical errors. Sometimes it's hard to be respectful to adults, especially ones who may not be kind to you. Paul describes the people in a church as family, though. Paul assumes that we treat our own families with respect, love, and care. Paul talks about women whose husbands have died, leaving them all alone. But if these widows have family, they will be taken care of. Consider verse 8 when it comes to taking care of brothers, sisters, and other members of your family.

How do you treat your brothers and sisters? Is it honoring to God? Do you honor and care for your parents and grandparents?

Tuesday · 1 TIMOTHY 5:9-16

Q

A

DIGGING DEEPER • So what's the big deal with widows? It was a big deal at this church. If a widow didn't have any family, the church was supposed to take care of her. This included food, water, housing, medicine, and everything else. Some widows could have just been looking for free help. It was pretty common for people to lose their health, die young, or get diseases in those days. Timothy needed these guidelines so that he could encourage the church to take care of the widows who needed the most help. Some people try and get free stuff instead of working for it. Families need to take care of their own, instead of looking for short-cuts.

Are you always trying to get out of your home responsibilities? Do you work hard and take care of yourself, or do you expect your parents to do everything?

Wednesday · 1 Timothy 5:17-25

Q

A

DIGGING DEEPER • Paul now gives Timothy some advice about the other pastors at the church. Faithful pastors deserve special honor. What's up with the ox? It may sound gross, but oxen walked over and crushed the grain so that it could be used for cooking. The point is, if the ox is crushing the grain, let him eat some while he's working. He deserves it. Likewise, make sure the pastor is taken care of financially and physically. He works for the Lord! Paul tells Timothy to take a little wine as medicine. That doesn't mean it's OK to drink, though. Medicine is far more advanced today. Timothy was a faithful pastor and would never consider using alcohol in a way that would be offensive to others or harmful to his body.
Would you be willing to do something special for your pastor to show him honor? Would you commit to praying for him and his difficult job?

Thursday · 1 Timothy 6:1-8

Q

A

DIGGING DEEPER • Slavery? Whoa! In the Bible? This actually isn't the same kind of slavery you might think of. First, these people were more like workers. But Paul did want to make sure the relationship between the two Christians was correct. Check out Ephesians 6:7-9 for more understanding. Secondly, are you happy? Do you feel like you need something else to make you happy? Verse 7 means that godly people will be content and satisfied, no matter what they have. These false teachers were always after "more." The point is, we can be completely satisfied with Christ alone. Does He still bless us? Yes! And for that we can be grateful, thankful, and content with what we have.
Are you a faithful worker? Do you always do your best? Are you willing to be satisfied with what you have? What really should bring you happiness?

Friday · 1 TIMOTHY 6:9-16

Q

A

DIGGING DEEPER · What's valuable to you? Verses 9-10 or 15-16? Money or the Messiah? That should be an easy question to answer. At least we know the right answer, but is the right answer really true of us? All those characteristics of God in verse 15-16 are so magnificent! Does it thrill you to know you have an intimate, close relationship with that person? WOW! Maybe you just want to have money. Having money isn't wrong, but the key is found in verse 10. What do you love: Money or the Messiah? God or goodies? The benefits of the Messiah and the downfalls of money are really clear in this passage.

What do you spend your time thinking about most? What do you spend your time pursuing the most? Straight up: what or whom do you love?

Saturday · 1 TIMOTHY 6:17-21

Q

A

DIGGING DEEPER · Do you want to be rich? Actually, you *can* be. But the question is, what is important to you in the future? Where is your hope? If it is in God, He can still bless you here on earth, even for your enjoyment. Not only that— He wants you to be rich in good deeds. If your treasure is here on this earth, you may get it, but it won't last. *Or...* you could be rich in good deeds and, by giving, send your treasure on ahead of you to enjoy for *eternity!* Part of the key is being content with what you have (v. 6) and being faithful to the Lord in your actions. It's easy to look at what your friends have, and want to be rich now, but why not leave that up to the Lord? He'll give you what you need now, and bless you for eternity!

What believer could you share with? How can you change your focus from being rich now to being rich in eternity?

QuietTime

WEEK 8

Oh great...Leviticus! Many will say that this book of instruction and law is written for the old culture, but they are wrong. You will see how alive this book is, with full application for today. This week is all about how sinful people are able to approach a holy God... so get with it!

Prayer focus for this week

THE QUESTION · *What is the writer saying?*
THE ANSWER · *How Can I apply this to my life?*

Sunday · LEVITICUS 1:1-9

Q
A

DIGGING DEEPER · If it were up to you, what would you come up with to take away the sins of the world? What would be your gospel? What about sin? Today, we see that God had a plan that would allow us to come to Him and to deal with our sin. Why a male? Because Jesus was a male. Why a lamb? Because Jesus was the Lamb of God. Why blood? Because Jesus shed His blood on the cross for us to atone for our sin. Why was the smell "sweet" to God? Because it satisfied the righteous demands of a holy God...Jesus, too, was a fragrant aroma because He satisfied the righteous demands of a holy God (2 Corinthians 2:15). **How did the Old Testament saints get saved? The whole sacrificial system pointed to the coming Messiah. Should you be pointing anyone to the Savior today with an appropriate witness?**

Monday · LEVITICUS 5:1-13

Q

A

DIGGING DEEPER • Where does repentance begin? It begins when you meet with God! The presence of God illuminates and reveals our sin so that we can see how we've missed the mark of God's perfection. God's Law reveals the truth that all have sinned and come short of God's glory. God has not only furnished the Law to reveal man's sin, He has furnished a way to pay the price for man's sin. Atonement must occur for sin to be removed. Christ did that for you! At some point, though, the process of repentance goes from God calling us, to our acceptance of God's call and provision for our forgiveness. We must turn from our sin and trust the fact that God has forgiven us. That's what is called victory over sin!

Can you trust that God has forgiven your sin? How do you know that God has forgiven your sins? What will break the pattern of sin in your life?

Tuesday · LEVITICUS 17:1-14

Q

A

DIGGING DEEPER • How many times did Jesus have to die on the cross to pay for the sins of the world? How many places did His blood have to be shed to make payment in full for all mankind's sin? According to these verses, blood is not food; it carries life and the value of sacrifice. The command of God that the sacrifice be made in His presence, in one place, pointed to the sufficiency of Calvary in every way. Jesus died in one place, on one cross; His blood was shed in one area. It was enough! To God, blood is a serious matter…now do you wonder why?

How are you treating the blood of Jesus in your life? Does it give you license to sin or a desire to serve? You should want to serve out of gratitude. Serving Him can begin today. Find a way!

Wednesday · LEVITICUS 19:9-18

Q

A

DIGGING DEEPER • Is "holy" a verb? It means to be set apart AND it is something we are called to live out as an action every day. Looking at the list of these written laws, there are a lot of "Thou shalt nots." So is God a cosmic killjoy? Every one of God's laws points to living a life that is set apart from the ways of this world. God does not intend to ruin our lives or keep us from having fun. He desires to bring us to a place of living by faith and abundance through His laws and provisions. Imagine what would happen if God did not supply boundaries for living. It would be chaos. Everyone would make up his own rules. This is called anarchy.

How do God's laws affect your life? Do you see them as valuable or a hindrance? Is it worth following God's laws? How about working on the ones listed in v. 11 – stealing or lying? It would be a great start for victory.

Thursday · LEVITICUS 20:6-10; 22-27

Q

A

DIGGING DEEPER • Would you go swimming in a pond next to a sign that said "DANGER, DO NOT SWIM – ALLIGATORS!"? It's a no-brainer...you wouldn't go swimming. As a matter of fact, you would be glad someone took the time to make the sign and put it there to warn you. God's Law is purposed to keep us alive and blessed because He has a plan for our lives. He wants us to live a life full of blessings so we can receive what He has in store for those who abide in Him. What's weird is that there is always someone who still wants to jump in the pond and disregard the warning. Departing from the Law is a deadly thing. The Law is not legalism when the purpose is to protect and prosper those who follow it.

Have you been swimming with alligators lately? Maybe you're taking God's patience and grace for granted. It's time to get out of the pond, NOW!

Friday · LEVITICUS 22:17-25

Q

A

DIGGING DEEPER • What does God deserve from you? Are you offering God the best, or leftovers from your life? Christ gave His very best and all that He had. He was perfect, without blemish, like the offerings in this passage were supposed to be. They depicted the future sacrifice of Christ. Do you arrive tired and late to Sunday morning Bible Study? What about your church attendance? Does your job or recreation time take precedence over time for worship on Sunday? You say, "Hey, I give God Wednesdays and I tithe, too." Do your friends get more devotion from you than God does? God calls this unacceptable. He requires and is due the first fruits of your life. Imagine if God gave to you the way you give to Him. **What are you giving to God as an offering of your life? Is He getting the first fruits, or just leftovers?**

Saturday · LEVITICUS 23:4-14

Q

A

DIGGING DEEPER • Have you ever played basketball by just hanging a rim on a pole with no backboard? Probably not. It's amazing how helpful the backboard is. It gives you better perception, a target, and a place to bank your shots. The Old Testament is like the backboard, and the New Testament is like the rim. You can make it with just the New Testament, but having the Old Testament makes it a lot easier. It helps us see the BIG picture of redemption. These verses helped Israel understand the role of the Messiah, since they would not see Him, and what it meant to trust God's promise of redemption sealed by the blood of a lamb. They could remember how God fulfills His every promise. **Do you remember to praise God for saving you from your sin? Does He have to remind you? At your next meal, why not thank Him for salvation?**

QuietTime

Forgotten anything today? Need a Post-it Note on your forehead? How often do you think about the day God saved you from your sin? Does God have to remind you, or do you stay in a constant state of gratitude for what He has done?

WEEK 9

Prayer focus for this week

THE QUESTION *What is the writer saying?*
THE ANSWER *How Can I apply this to my life?*

Sunday · LEVITICUS 23:15-22

Q

A

DIGGING DEEPER · How did people in the Old Testament get saved? Did God change the rules in the New Testament? Think about it…Christ had not been born yet. He hadn't died yet, and hadn't risen from the dead yet. If you look closely at these verses, you can see that everything represents an aspect of Christ as Savior and His role as Messiah. For example, the time between festivals is 50 days, right? The time between Christ rising again and Pentecost was exactly 50 days! There is symbolism and prophecy written in every order of worship in these verses. Look for more yourself. The Old Testament people were saved the very same way we are…through the blood of the Lamb. **Are you relying on Christ for your salvation as much today as the day you were saved? Remember, Christ is ALL that we need.**

Monday · LEVITICUS 23:23-32

Q

A

DIGGING DEEPER • Wouldn't it be cool to practice for the Rapture—hearing the trumpet and getting ready for the ride of your life? Leviticus 23:24 ties into the Rapture of the church and the prophecy of Christ's return. Notice that these instructions aren't just for feasts of feeding God's people; they are for gathering His people. As a coach blows his whistle to get his team together, Christ will one day descend with a shout and with the trumpet of God to gather His people (1 Thessalonians 4:16). When the trumpet sounds, the dead in Christ will rise first and then the living believers will be caught up in the air. What a meeting that is going to be!

Are you worried about Christ coming because you don't want to miss out on stuff here? Maybe it's time to remember that this world wasn't built to last! Is your life and all you're about fireproof?

Tuesday · LEVITICUS 23:33-44

Q

A

DIGGING DEEPER • Remember when? Have you had some times when you're just hanging out with friends and start thinking about memories, blasts from the past where some incredible stuff happened? Some were good, some bad, some really funny...but you remember them because they were unique and special. God had ordered His people to celebrate when He delivered them from bondage in Egypt and provided for them all along the way to Canaan. Isn't it a shame that God has to make us remember what He has done for us? But He knows our nature and He understands our weakness.

Thank God for the instruction He gives us in spite of our selfishness. Consider God's patience today in light of how you treat Him. Do you remember all He has done for you?

Wednesday · LEVITICUS 25:1-17

Q

A

DIGGING DEEPER • Ask a farmer why he gives seasons of "rest" to some of his land, and he'll tell you it's to replenish the soil so it will strengthen his harvest in years to come. He may not know it, but he's proving a biblical principle. Why would God want us to observe a day of each week as a day of rest? God rested a full day after He finished creating the world and man. God has ordered a day to be set aside to focus on what God has done: a day of worship! The Sabbath was Saturday because it was the last day of the week. Sunday has always been the first day of the week. We celebrate the Lord's day now on Sunday because it was the day that Jesus rose from the grave, the first day of the week.

When was the last time you "rested" on the Lord's Day and really focused on His goodness? Maybe that's why your harvest isn't so good!

Thursday · LEVITICUS 26:3-17

Q

A

DIGGING DEEPER • Who's your hero? In a recent homework assignment, out of 300 elementary school students, only one put Jesus Christ as his hero! Sports stars, musicians, actors, and politicians were the heroes for everyone else. In these verses today, God has made a command that demands our attention and obedience. He IS Lord! Maybe that's the key to our country returning to God; stop with the recreation and sports as our god and return our hearts to Him. God promised the Israelites that if they obeyed they would be blessed but if they disobeyed, God would punish severely. Those who trust in Christ have the promise of eternal life, and our obedience to God determines our abundance in Christ.

Who's your hero? Look on the walls of your room...or in the CD player. Are sports, cheerleading, a new car, and your friends put before God?

Friday · LEVITICUS 26:18-31

Q

A

DIGGING DEEPER · How serious is God about being Lord? How serious are you in your own life about it? God promised the Israelites a blessed land and life if they would abide in His laws. God also promised punishment if they did not abide by His laws. When God commanded these words to be written, He wasn't laughing and hoping the people would mess up. He deserves to be obeyed because He is God. Today God promises to discipline those who are going astray (Hebrews 12:5-11). You may not like it, but He IS God! Just as God made it clear how a person can have eternal life, He also made it clear how we are to live. It's not a guessing game at all. He proved His love by writing it down for us to know.

Do you consider anything God says about punishment to be unreasonable? Do you respect God's discipline as you should?

Saturday · LEVITICUS 26:32-46

Q

A

DIGGING DEEPER · If God were as faithful to you as you are to Him, how would life be? God promised the Israelites that if they sinned He would not forget them forever, but that He would remember His promises and restore them. It's time to understand something very real...if you do not abide in God's commands, God will not bless your life. It's amazing how much we want to fight God over this principle, not necessarily with words, but with actions. Actually, our obedience is really an issue of trust. Information becomes understanding when you live out what you know to be true. Notice that when you return to God, the effect of sin still must be worked out. The difference is that God is with you every step of the way.

How has God walked with you through the effects of your disobedience once you turned to Him?

QuietTime

Do you like a lot of action? If so, you will like this week's passage. There are confrontations with Satan and demons, fishing on dry land, miracles, a party, and a plot to kill the Son of God. How much more action could you ask for?

Prayer focus for this week

THE QUESTION   *What is the writer saying?*
THE ANSWER   *How Can I apply this to my life?*

Sunday · MARK 1:1-13

Q

A

DIGGING DEEPER • The Gospel of Mark is intended to share the good news of "Jesus Christ, the Son of God." John the Baptist came before Christ as predicted by prophets in the Old Testament. He prepared people for Christ's arrival by preaching repentance from sin. John acted and dressed differently than most people, yet his primary difference was how he treated Jesus. John put Jesus ahead of himself. The Trinity appears at the baptism when God the Spirit descends like a dove and God the Father speaks, revealing that Jesus is God the Son. Immediately afterward, Jesus goes into the wilderness to be tempted by Satan for forty days. Following Jesus' temptation, God sends angels to care for Him. **Are you sharing the good news of Jesus Christ? Do Jesus and His plans come before yours? Are you aware that God's angels take care of you, too?**

Monday · MARK 1:14-28

Q
A

DIGGING DEEPER • Do you like to fish? If so, how big was your biggest catch? Jesus called His first disciples, or followers. They were fishermen, and He challenged them to "be-come fishers of men." They immediately gave up their fishing business to follow Him. On Saturday, Jesus went to a synagogue, or Jewish place of worship, to teach. His teaching was not like the other teachers'. He taught with authority, and those who heard Him were astonished. Then He amazed them by casting a demon out of a man. As a result, Jesus quickly became famous in that area.
Have you accepted the challenge to become a fisher of men, winning others to Christ? What are you willing to give up to follow Him? Do you recognize and submit to the authority of God's teaching through the Bible?

Tuesday · MARK 1:29-35

Q
A

DIGGING DEEPER • Jesus and the disciples went to Simon Peter's house. His mother-in-law was sick with a fever, and Jesus healed her. Immediately, she began serving and waiting on them as if she had never been sick. That evening, the people of the city brought all the sick and demon possessed to Him. He healed the sick and cast out the demons. The next morning, Jesus got up before daylight and went off by Himself to pray. If the sinless Son of God felt the need to spend quality time with the Father in prayer, then we, too, should spend time with Him in prayer. Consistent prayer gives us the power to serve God each day.
Are you serving the Lord who healed you from the guilt of your sins? Do you spend quality time by yourself in prayer? Is your Quiet Time an essential part of every day? Is your Quiet Time quite a time?

Wednesday · Mark 1:36-45

DIGGING DEEPER • While Jesus was away praying, a large crowd came to see Him. Peter went to find Him, to explain that many were seeking Him. However, Jesus was ready to go and preach in other towns, because that was what He came to do. He would not be distracted from His plan. As Jesus went on His way preaching, a leper came to Him for healing. At that time, lepers were outcasts and no one would even touch them, yet our Lord had compassion on him. He reached out His hand, touched the leper, and healed him. Today there are outcast people in our society—those to whom no one wants to reach out. We should have compassion, reach out, and tell them the good news of Jesus Christ.

Are you focused on what God would have you do, or are you easily distracted? Do you have compassion for the outcasts of our society?

Thursday · Mark 2:1-12

DIGGING DEEPER • When Jesus returned to Capernaum, a large crowd gathered to see Him. As always, He began preaching to them. Preaching was a major priority in His life. Miracles, like the one in this passage, proved that His message was true. Four men brought a paralyzed friend to Him for healing. Due to the large crowd, no one could get in through the door, so they lowered their friend through the roof. Jesus, seeing their faith, forgave the paralyzed man his sins. Next, because of the religious leaders' unbelief, Jesus healed the man. Immediately, he stood up, picked up his bed, and walked out. Everyone was amazed and began to glorify God.

Do you recognize the importance of preaching? What will you do to bring a friend to Jesus? If difficulties arise will you overcome them?

Friday · MARK 2:13-28

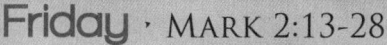

DIGGING DEEPER • Levi, a despised tax collector for Rome, obeyed Jesus' command to follow Him. He had a gathering of friends, and Jesus and His disciples ate with them. The religious leaders questioned Jesus for eating with these despised people. Yet Jesus came to die for sinners such as this. Like Him, we should separate ourselves from sin but not from "sinners." They also questioned Him about fasting and keeping the Sabbath. In both situations, Jesus and His disciples were not breaking the Old Testament law, but traditions added by the religious leaders. The old garments and bottles represented Judaism and its laws. The new cloth and new bottles represent the Gospel.

Do you shun unbelievers or do you reach out to them with the Gospel? Are you bound by man-made traditions or set free by God's Word?

Saturday · MARK 3:1-12

DIGGING DEEPER • Because of their unbelief, the religious leaders began looking for a reason to arrest and kill Jesus. A man with a crippled hand was in the synagogue on the Sabbath day. Jesus entered, and the religious leaders saw an opportunity to trap Him. Knowing their intention, Jesus asked them whether it is lawful to do good or evil, save or kill, on the Sabbath. He was comparing His intention with theirs. Jesus intended to do good and save. They intended to do evil and kill. When they refused to admit this, Jesus became angry and saddened. It is right to be angry at sin and its effects. Later, people came from every direction to be healed. When demons recognized Him, Jesus refused to accept their witness.

Are the intentions of your heart to do good or evil? Does sin and its effects sadden you and make you angry? Do you have a problem with anger?

QuietTime

Have you ever been a member of a club or group which you really enjoyed, and from which you learned a lot? Maybe it was scouts, band, or a sports team. Groups like these often change the direction of people's lives. This week Jesus forms a small group of men whom He will teach how to change their world.

Prayer focus for this week

THE QUESTION   *What is the writer saying?*
THE ANSWER   *How Can I apply this to my life?*

Sunday · MARK 3:13-21

DIGGING DEEPER · Jesus asked several of His friends to climb a mountain with Him. While on the mountain, He selected twelve of them for two purposes: First, He chose them to be with Him. As simple as this may sound, Jesus knew it was the best way for them to learn of Him. Second, He chose them so He could send them out to preach. One of Jesus' priorities was preaching, and He wanted that to continue when He was gone. He also gave them the power to heal and cast out demons, so people would know they were with Him. These twelve men, except for Judas Iscariot, become those whom God used to start the Church. Sadly, some of His own friends misunderstood Him and thought He was crazy and tried to stop Him.

How much time do you spend with Jesus? Are you learning of Him? Do you proclaim His message? Have you been misunderstood by others?

Monday · MARK 3:22-35

Q

A

DIGGING DEEPER • A country or house working against itself will be destroyed. The religious leaders said that Satan controlled Jesus. But if Satan cast out his own demons, he would be working against himself. Also, to destroy a strong man's house, first the strong man (Satan) must be overpowered. The Holy Spirit cast out demons through Jesus to show that He was the Christ. By giving Satan credit, the leaders were rejecting the Spirit's witness to Jesus. To reject that witness is to never accept Jesus Christ as your personal savior, and to resist the convicting work of the Holy Spirit. Jesus declares that His family is not based on flesh and blood, but on obedience to the will of God. It is a spiritual family.
Are you aware that God controls all things, including Satan? When did you accept the Spirit's witness by trusting Jesus? Are you doing God's will?

Tuesday · MARK 4:1-12

Q

A

DIGGING DEEPER • Have you ever had a "secret code" for writing to friends so others could not understand? Jesus used parables in a similar way to reveal truth to believers while hiding it from those who refused to believe. Parables are stories about everyday situations used to teach spiritual truth. This story is about planting a field, and how the seeds grow in different types of soil. Jesus explained to the disciples that they, as believers, were going to find out what the parable meant. However, those who refused to believe would be kept from understanding, turning from their sin, and being forgiven. This parable is explained in tomorrow's verses.
Why do some people disbelieve our witness? If you know someone who has put off believing in Jesus, what should you do?

Q
A

DIGGING DEEPER • Witnessing is like planting in different kinds of soil. Some people have hard hearts and are easily misled by Satan. Some accept the witness with excitement but with no commitment, and leave when mistreated for being a Christian. Some accept but are distracted by responsibilities, money, or desires for other things and never make a difference. Finally, some will hear, accept, and make a difference. Only these are true Christians. The lamp or candle teaches that the truth should not be hidden but made known. The measure shows that as we live out the truth we will be given more truth. As with planting and harvesting, we witness and receive those who believe. As with growing plants, God does the work.

What kind of soil are you? Are you living out the truth God has taught you? What are your responsibilities in witnessing? What are God's?

Thursday · MARK 4:30-41

Q
A

DIGGING DEEPER • The mustard seed was the smallest garden seed in that part of the world, and was a small plant. However, it could grow into a fifteen-foot-tall monster plant. Likewise, the kingdom of God began small and grew normally in the early stages. Later, those who were not true believers attached themselves, causing it to grow abnormally. The birds represent those who are evil. Jesus and His disciples were crossing the Sea of Galilee when a storm began to sink their boat. The disciples showed their lack of faith in Jesus by panicking. Jesus showed He was God by calming the storm with just a word. The disciples were even more afraid. Which one would you rather have, a storm outside your boat or God inside your life?

Are you a true member of the kingdom? How can you recognize those who are evil? Do you respond to the storms in your life with panic or with faith?

Friday · MARK 5:1-10

Q

A

DIGGING DEEPER • Today some people are obsessed with the supernatural—everything from ghosts to psychics. Jesus showed His power over the supernatural by helping a man possessed by demons. Tortured constantly, the man lived in tombs or burial caves, screamed all the time, and cut himself with stones. Nobody was able to help him. When they tried to restrain him, he broke free with demonic strength. Only Jesus can help men controlled by sin and Satan. These demons called themselves Legion, the name for a group of two-to six-thousand Roman soldiers. Recognizing Jesus as the Son of God, they begged Him not to throw them out of the area. They knew He had power to do whatever He wanted with them.
Do you believe that only Jesus can deal with sin and Satan? Is there anyone beyond His help? Can any number of demons win over Jesus?

Saturday · MARK 5:11-20

Q

A

DIGGING DEEPER • Ever want to be a pig? Probably not, but these demons did. Whatever Jesus had in store for them, being a pig had to be better. When possessed, the pigs drowned themselves immediately. What a shocking picture of the consequences of evil. As people gathered, they saw the man acting normally. They became afraid of the person who had overpowered thousands of demons, just as the disciples had after He calmed the storm. Because of their fear, they asked Jesus to leave their area. In contrast, the man who was healed wanted to go with Jesus. Jesus told him to tell his family and friends about the great things God had done for him and how much mercy he had received. The man went and did just that.
What are some of the consequences of evil? Does Jesus' power drive you away from or toward Him? Are there family and friends you have not told?

QuietTime

Sometimes it seems like getting respect from close friends and family is too difficult. Those who have known us from childhood often cannot see how we have grown up. Take heart! Jesus had the same problem. Fewer people took him seriously in His own hometown than in any other place in which He ministered.

Prayer focus for this week

THE QUESTION · *What is the writer saying?*

THE ANSWER · *How Can I apply this to my life?*

Sunday · MARK 5:21-34

Q

A

DIGGING DEEPER · A ruler of the synagogue came for help with his dying daughter. Most religious leaders hated Jesus and wanted to kill Him, yet this man needed Him. Times of difficulty often make people realize their need for Jesus. While Jesus was on His way to the girl, a woman touched Him for healing. The woman had been sick for twelve years. None of the doctors could help her. She was out of money, out of options and getting worse. Jesus, however, was able to heal her instantly. Many people touched Him in that crowd, but only one person touched Him in faith. As a result, she received healing, peace, and freedom from suffering. Faith causes God's power to be shown. He loves to show His power in response to our faith.
When was the last time you shared God's love with a person in need? What are you trusting God for that only His power can accomplish?

Monday · MARK 5:35-43

Q

A

DIGGING DEEPER • Has needed help ever come too little and too late? Jesus was still talking to the woman He healed when word came of the girl's death. Her father must have been disappointed. Jesus told him to trust and not be afraid. As He went to the girl, only His inner circle was allowed to follow. These men were being trained to lead when Jesus was gone. Upon arrival, He asked why they were mourning a sleeping girl. They laughed at Him because they knew she was dead. Jesus said "sleep" because He knew she would wake from the dead. No matter how things appear, God's help is never too little or too late. Jesus often told people not to talk about His miracles. His preaching was more important.

When difficulty comes, do you fear the problem or trust in God? Do you let appearances shake your faith? List times when God's help was just right.

Tuesday · MARK 6:1-13

Q

A

DIGGING DEEPER • Jesus visited His hometown. His wisdom in teaching and power to heal surprised them. Some became upset because they had known Him and His family since He was a child. They had a hard time accepting Jesus as the Son of God. In turn, He was surprised by their unbelief, and because of it, only a few miracles were performed. For the first time, Jesus sent out the twelve disciples to preach. Sent in pairs, they could encourage and protect each other. To prove that their message was true, Jesus gave them power to cast out demons and to heal the sick. They were told to travel light, trusting God to supply their needs. Shaking dust off their feet showed that they rejected those who rejected God's message.

Are you limiting what God can do in your life by unbelief? With whom can you partner for witnessing? Do you trust God to supply your needs?

Wednesday · MARK 6:14-29

DIGGING DEEPER • There was controversy over who Jesus was. Some said He was John the Baptist raised from the dead; some, the Old Testament prophet Elijah; and some, a brand new prophet. Since King Herod had ordered John the Baptist killed, he was frightened, thinking that Jesus was John the Baptist raised from the dead. Herod was married to his brother's ex-wife, who was also his niece. John had told Herod the marriage was sinful and wrong. After that, Herod's wife, Herodias, hated John and wanted to kill him because he confronted her sin. She used her daughter to trick Herod into killing John. The king made a foolish promise and a more foolish mistake by keeping it. He allowed peer pressure to control him.

Are you confronting sin? How do you react when your sin is confronted? Should a foolish promise be kept? Are you controlled by peer pressure?

Thursday · MARK 6:30-44

DIGGING DEEPER • When we're away from home and hungry we can find a fast-food place, but not so in Jesus' day. The disciples returned from their first preaching trip and re-ported to Jesus. They were tired, so He sent them away for rest; but a large crowd followed along. Rather than being irritated by the interruption, Jesus had compassion and taught them. The disciples wanted to send the people away for supper, but Jesus said to feed them. To provide enough food for the crowd would have cost eight month's salary. Jesus miraculously fed them with five loaves of bread and two fish. Afterward, twelve baskets of leftovers were picked up, perhaps one for each of the faithless disciples.

When have you become tired working for God? How well do you handle interruptions? Do you trust God to do things not humanly possible?

Friday · MARK 6:45-56

Q

A

DIGGING DEEPER •   Jesus sent the disciples away by boat while He prayed alone. Strong winds were giving the disciples trouble in the boat. After praying till 3 a.m., Jesus walked across the water to the boat. Thinking He was a ghost, the disciples were afraid. When He got into the boat the wind stopped. Even after seeing the food miracle, they were shocked by Jesus walking on water and calming the storm. Their hard hearts kept them from knowing that Jesus was God. As with the disciples then, Jesus is praying for us and helping us today. When the boat landed, sick people flocked to Jesus and He completely and instantly healed many.
When was the last time you prayed till 3 a.m.? For 3 hours? For 3 minutes? How have Jesus' miracles affected your faith in Him?

Saturday · MARK 7:1-13

Q

A

DIGGING DEEPER •   Would you eat on dirty dishes with unwashed hands? Of course not, and neither would Jesus and the disciples. Isaiah prophesied that the Jews would outwardly worship God but not really love Him, and that they would make up their own teachings to replace His. The matter here is not that the disciples' hands were dirty. Rather, they had not engaged in the ritualistic tradition of the Pharisees and scribes. Jesus condemned the Pharisees and scribes for keeping their traditions while breaking God's Word. For example, God said we are to respect and take care of our parents, but they used their made-up teaching to avoid doing what God taught in the Bible.
Do you truly love God or just put on a show? What man-made traditions do you put ahead of God's Word? How do you show honor to your parents?

Have you ever tried to do something you have done before, but now it just will not work? Several people are watching, and the harder you try the more trouble you have. Then someone comes along and easily does it, making you look foolish. This week the disciples find themselves in a similar situation.

Prayer focus for this week

THE QUESTION *What is the writer saying?*
THE ANSWER *How Can I apply this to my life?*

Sunday · MARK 7:14-23

DIGGING DEEPER · Ever gotten sick from a stomach virus, and then blamed it on the last thing you ate and avoided that food for months? The real problem was already inside, but the food was blamed by mistake. Similarly, the religious leaders believed they were pure on the inside and needed to keep outside things from corrupting them, like certain foods, people, places, and objects. Jesus taught just the opposite-that people are corrupted by what is inside them. Sin in our heart corrupts us. Sin inside produces the sinful desires and actions that come out. Adultery and fornication are sexual sins in and out of marriage. Lasciviousness or lewdness is wild and shameless sinful living. Malice or wickedness is hurtful actions and words.
Are you dealing with your sinful heart or blaming other things? How well are you dealing with each sin listed in this passage?

Monday · MARK 7:24-37

Q

A

DIGGING DEEPER · Jesus leaves Jewish Galilee and travels to a Gentile area, possibly trying to get time alone with His disciples. A Gentile woman asks Jesus to cast a demon out of her daughter. He responds with an analogy. The children's (Jews') food (God's blessing) should not be given to pet dogs (Gentiles) that will be fed (Gospel) later. She could have been offended and left in a huff. Yet, her response showed faith and humility. As a result, her daughter was healed. After Jesus moved on from there, a deaf man who could not speak was brought to Him. After touching the man's ears and tongue, Jesus healed him with a command. Truly, He does all things well!

Are you easily offended by the truth in God's Word or do you submit in faith and humility? What has the Lord done well for you? Give thanks.

Tuesday · MARK 8:1-10

Q

A

DIGGING DEEPER · Another large crowd gathered in the desert to hear Jesus teach. After three days of teaching, the people were out of food and hungry. Without food they would not be able to travel back home. Jesus cared about their physical needs and wanted to feed them. Amazingly, the disciples questioned how they could feed such a large crowd. Had they forgotten how He fed five thousand with five loaves and two fish? Nevertheless, they doubted Him. After He fed them with seven loaves and a few fish, seven large baskets full of leftovers were gathered. The Greek word implies that these baskets were much larger than the twelve before.

How many meals would you miss to learn God's Word? Are you concerned about people's physical needs? Have you forgotten God's past provision?

Wednesday · MARK 8:11-26

DIGGING DEEPER • Has anyone ever asked you to do something just to make you look bad? The Pharisees asked Jesus to perform a sign because they did not think He could. He refused because they had rejected all His previous miracles. As they were leaving, Jesus warned the disciples about the leaven or yeast of the Pharisees and Herod. Leaven in the Bible refers to sin and evil. Their sin was rejecting and trying to destroy Jesus. Somehow, after two bread miracles, the disciples thought there was not enough bread. The blind man's two-part healing was a lesson for the disciples. His eyes were first made blurry, and then made clear. Likewise, the disciples' spiritual eyes were blurry but would soon be made clear. **Have you tested God by asking for a sign? Do you have the "leaven" of the Pharisees and Herod? If so, repent! Are your spiritual eyes clear or blurry?**

Thursday · MARK 8:27-38

DIGGING DEEPER • There was controversy about who Jesus was. Peter and the disciples realized He was the Christ, their Savior, promised in the Old Testament. Yet they thought He would be king, and save them from their enemies instead of their sins. When Jesus said that the religious leaders would kill Him, Peter rebuked Him. A king should not talk that way. Jesus told Peter he was speaking Satan's words and thinking selfishly. Then Jesus told the people that they must be willing to give up everything, even their life, to be His disciples. To have true abundant life, we must give our whole lives to God. If we are ashamed of Him now, then He will be ashamed of us when He comes back. **Who do you say Jesus is? Is your thinking controlled by Satan or God? Are you willing to give your life to God, or are you ashamed of Him?**

Friday · MARK 9:1-13

DIGGING DEEPER • We all like sneak previews. Jesus promised that some people with Him would see God's kingdom before they died. A few days later, He gave His closest disciples a look at the kingdom. They saw Jesus shining bright with power. He was whiter than snow. Moses and Elijah represented the Law and Prophets—two major parts of the Old Testament. Peter's suggestion to build three tents or shelters for them put Moses and Elijah on the same level as Jesus. God the Father put Jesus above them by saying that Jesus was His Son. Jesus told the disciples to keep quiet because they would not understand what happened until after He came back from the dead. **Are you looking forward to seeing God's kingdom yourself? Do you listen to Jesus above all other men? Do you understand before speaking?**

Saturday · MARK 9:14-29

DIGGING DEEPER • The disciples were having trouble casting a demon out of a boy. This is odd, be-cause Jesus had already given them the power to cast out demons. When Jesus heard of the problem, He rebuked them for their lack of faith. This demon was violent and had tried to kill the boy many times. After rebuking them all for unbelief, Jesus tells the father that his child can be cured if he will believe that Jesus can cure him. The father realized his belief was mixed with doubt, and wisely asked Jesus to help him. Jesus did and cured the boy. He told the disciples they failed because they trusted themselves rather than trusting God through prayer and fasting. *Fasting* means to stop eating for a time so one can focus on God. **Is your faith lacking? Have you asked God to increase your faith and dependence on Him? Do you show your trust in God by daily prayer?**

QuietTime

WEEK
14

At your age, you are probably putting a lot of effort into proving you are not a child anymore, especially if you've been told to "grow up." Ironically, Jesus says you must accept His kingdom as a little child if you want to get in. This week you will find out what He meant.

Prayer focus for this week

THE QUESTION · *What is the writer saying?*
THE ANSWER · *How Can I apply this to my life?*

Sunday · MARK 9:30-41

DIGGING DEEPER · Sometimes we are afraid to ask a question because we are not sure we want to hear the answer. When Jesus told the disciples that He would die and rise from the dead on the third day, they were afraid to ask what this meant. Desire for power and greatness causes many to serve themselves rather than God. To be great, Jesus says we must serve other people rather than be served by them. He gives a humble child as an example of the right attitude, in contrast with the proud arguing of the disciples. The disciples rebuked a man working in Jesus' name just because he was not part of their group. Jesus replied that everyone truly serving God is part of their group.

Are there questions you are afraid to ask God? How do you seek greatness? How do you treat God's servants in other groups?

Monday · MARK 9:42-50

Q

A

DIGGING DEEPER • Causing a believer to sin, especially a small child, is a very serious issue. Jesus says it would be better to have a big rock tied around your neck and to be thrown in deep water to drown. Also, Jesus is serious about us dealing with our own sin. To show how serious the effects of sin are, He says we would be better off without our hand, foot, and eye than to fall into sin. Of course, He does not mean that we should cut off body parts to deal with sin. Sin is a spiritual problem and must be dealt with by the Bible and prayer. Verse 49 refers to the consequences of sin–difficulty in this life, death, eternal Hell, and separation from God. Salt was used to keep food from spoiling, and we should be salt for our spoiling society.
Have you ever caused a Christian to fall? If so, what are you doing about it? Do you deal with your sin? How are you being salt in your society?

Tuesday · MARK 10:1-16

Q

A

DIGGING DEEPER • Divorce is a big problem. The religious leaders tried to trick Jesus with their questions. Jesus quoted the Word, and then explained it by making four points about divorce. One, divorce was only permitted not commanded. Two, divorce was only allowed because of their stubborn and sinful hearts, but it was not the will of God. Three, a husband and wife become one person and should never be separated. Four, when someone divorces and remarries, he commits adultery against his original spouse. Unlike the disciples, Jesus allowed the children to come to Him. Only those who come in childlike faith and trust will be accepted by Him.
Do you go to the Bible for answers? What are some recent answers you got from the Bible? Have you stood in the way of people coming to Christ?

Wednesday · MARK 10:17-31

Q

A

DIGGING DEEPER · The man called Jesus "good" in his question, and only God is good. Jesus asked why he called Him good, since he did not believe Jesus was God. Jesus told him he must be perfect to get eternal life. The man thought he was perfect, but Jesus knew his heart and challenged his sin of greed. It can be difficult for a rich person to be saved because he depends on himself and his riches. It is impossible for anyone, rich or poor, to be saved on his own. But God can save anyone who depends on Him alone for salvation. All who give up everything for Jesus will be blessed in this life and in eternal life to come. Those who appear to be first now may end up last in Heaven, because God values different things.
Do you believe Jesus is God? Why? What do you really depend on in your life? Are you willing to give up all you have for all God has to offer?

Thursday · MARK 10:32-45

Q

A

DIGGING DEEPER · The final week of Jesus' life begins as He travels to Jerusalem. The disciples are amazed that He is fearlessly going to His death. For the third and final time, Jesus tells the twelve that He will die and rise again on the third day. The details are amazing. While Jesus selflessly goes to His death for the sin of the world, the disciples selfishly look out for themselves. James and John want to be ranked second and third in the kingdom. The cup and baptism Jesus asks about refer to His suffering and death for sin. He promises James and John that they will suffer and die for Him, but does not promise the rank they desire. Jesus reminds the disciples that greatness in His kingdom comes by serving, not by ruling.
How will you approach your death? Why? Are you motivated by desire for rank, position, and honor? Do you serve yourself or others?

Friday · MARK 10:46-52

Q
A

DIGGING DEEPER • Do you know that everyone is born blind? We are all born spiritually blind be-cause of sin. The blind man was begging beside a busy road. Because there was no work for blind people in those days, they had to beg for a living. Realizing Jesus was near, he called for help. When told to be quiet, he yelled even louder. Jesus stopped and asked what he wanted. He simply asked to receive the ability to see. Jesus healed him because of his faith, and he followed Jesus. Spiritually, we are all blind and poor. When Jesus is near we must call for help, not allowing anyone to stop us. In faith we must ask Him to heal us from our blindness. Then we must follow Him.

Have you received your spiritual sight by placing your faith in Jesus to save you from sin? If so, are you following Him?

Saturday · MARK 11:1-11

Q
A

DIGGING DEEPER • The guest of honor in a parade usually rides on a float or in the back of a convertible. Jesus rode into Jerusalem on a young donkey that had never been ridden. The Jews believed animals that had not been ridden should be used for holy purposes. Laying clothes on the road was a custom for welcoming a new king. The palm branches symbolized joy and salvation (Revelation 7:9-10). *Hosanna* means "save us now," and was used as a shout of praise, like *Hallelujah*. By referring to "the kingdom of our father David," the crowd recognized Jesus as the Messiah, the prophesied son of David. When Jesus got to Jerusalem, He went into the temple and gave it an inspection, since He is the great High Priest.

Does Jesus receive the place of honor in your life? Is He your King? Your body is the temple of the Holy Spirit. Would it pass Jesus' inspection?

QuietTime

WEEK 15

Have you ever had a teacher who liked to give at least one trick question on every test? These questions are designed to make you read all the questions carefully. In this passage, Jesus is tested with trick questions and passes with flying colors.

Prayer focus for this week

THE QUESTION   *What is the writer saying?*
THE ANSWER   *How Can I apply this to my life?*

Sunday · MARK 11:12-24

DIGGING DEEPER · Today, some people use religion as a means to steal money. The same was true in Jesus' day. A certain type of money was required to make offerings at the temple. The moneychangers had turned the temple into a great moneymaking business, and did not care about the purpose or intent of the sacrifices. This angered Jesus, and He cast them out of the temple. Normally, a fig tree produces figs before it develops all its leaves. Jesus cursed the tree because it had leaves, but no fruit. This was a picture of phony Israel, which looked spiritual but was not. Prayer and faith are a powerful combination. Whatever we ask in faith will be done, even moving a mountain.

As the temple of the Holy Spirit, what corruption do you need to clean out of your life? Are you a phony Christian? What has your prayer moved?

Monday · MARK 11:25-33

Q

A

DIGGING DEEPER · Not forgiving others negatively affects our prayer life. In fact, if we do not forgive others, then God will not forgive us. We are to forgive anything, whether big or small offenses. We are to forgive anybody, including believers and unbelievers. The religious leaders asked Jesus where He got the authority to clear out the temple, teach, and perform miracles. He knew they were trying to trap Him, so He asked them where John the Baptist got his authority. Both John and Jesus got their authority from God. If the religious leaders were willing to recognize John's authority, then they must recognize His, and He would answer them. Of course, their sinful hearts were not willing to recognize either one's authority.
What grudges are you holding? When are you going to forgive them? Do you recognize the Lord's authority? Are you submitting to it?

Tuesday · MARK 12:1-12

Q

A

DIGGING DEEPER · Jesus speaks to the religious leaders in parables— everyday stories that reveal spiritual truth. In the first parable, the man who planted the vineyard is God the Father. Those hired to care for the vineyard are the religious leaders. The servants that are mistreated and killed are the Old Testament prophets. The only Son is Jesus Christ, whom they kill out of greed. The Father destroying the wicked men and giving the vineyard to others foretells the laying aside of Israel and the rise of the church made up mostly of Gentiles. In the second parable, Jesus is the stone and the religious leaders are the builders. They reject Him by killing Him, but He rises to become the cornerstone of the Church.
Instead of repenting, the leaders rejected Jesus. Have you experienced rejection because of Jesus? If not, are you telling others about Him?

Wednesday · MARK 12:13-27

DIGGING DEEPER • Sometimes we are fooled by trick questions, but Jesus never was. The Pharisees and Herodians first flattered Him, and then asked about paying taxes to the Roman government. Everyone hated these taxes. If Jesus said to pay, the people would not like the answer. If He said not to pay, the government would not like the answer. Jesus' answer to pay Rome her taxes and give God His offerings stunned the questioners. Next, the Sadducees asked a question about the resurrection of the dead, in which they did not believe. The question was ridiculous, and Jesus pointed out two errors in their thinking: they were ignorant of the Scriptures, and they did not believe God had the power to raise people from the dead.

Do you recognize government's right to tax? Jesus did. What are you doing to learn the Scriptures? How much power do you believe God has?

Thursday · MARK 12:28-44

DIGGING DEEPER • Sometimes we get more than we ask for. A religious leader asked Jesus what was the most important command of God. His answer was to love God completely. He also gave the second most important command, which is to love your neighbor as yourself. The scribe agreed. Jesus answered the three questions so well, the leaders were afraid to ask any more. Next, He asked them one. How can Christ be both David's Son and his Lord? The answer is that He was both human, which the leaders believed, and God, which they did not believe. Jesus told His disciples not to be hypocrites like the leaders, who put on a show, but to be sincere like the widow, who gave everything.

Do you love God completely and other people like yourself? Do you make a big show to look spiritual? When have you given everything to God?

Friday · MARK 13:1-13

Q

A

DIGGING DEEPER • After Jesus predicted that the temple would be destroyed, the disciples wanted to know when it would happen and what the warning signs would be (this happened in 70 A.D.). They wrongly assumed the destruction of the temple would begin Jesus' kingdom on earth. Therefore, Jesus gave them the signs for the events that would occur before the establishment of His kingdom, during the Tribulation. The Tribulation begins after the Church is raptured, or taken up to Heaven, and lasts for seven years. During this time there will be false christs, wars, earth-quakes, famines, and all kinds of trouble. Jesus warns the disciples that they will be hated for His name's sake, yet the Holy Spirit will help them.
Are you looking forward to the Rapture? Do you get excited at the thought of God's kingdom? When were you hated because of Jesus?

Saturday · MARK 13:14-23

Q

A

DIGGING DEEPER • The "abomination of desolation" will happen in the middle of the seven-year Tribulation. At that time, the Antichrist will go into the rebuilt temple and demand to be worshiped. This is the beginning of the Great Tribulation. It will be the worst time in history. In fact, if God did not shorten the time, no one would be saved. The "elect" are the chosen of Israel, and they are told to get out of town immediately, without even taking time to pack. Women who are pregnant or have small children will have difficulty getting away. False christs will try to lure them out of hiding, but they should not be tricked, since Jesus has already warned them.
The living who have not trusted Christ as Savior will enter into the seven-year Tribulation and experience these things. Your opportunity to be saved will be BEFORE the Rapture. Have you trusted Him as Savior yet?

QuietTime

WEEK 16

Some of the best times in life are spent with close friends. Friends make us laugh and encourage us when we cry. But sometimes they let us down when we need them the most. In this week's passage, you will see how Jesus and His friends reacted during difficult times.

Prayer focus for this week

THE QUESTION — *What is the writer saying?*
THE ANSWER — *How Can I apply this to my life?*

Sunday · MARK 13:24-37

DIGGING DEEPER • In Friday's passage, the disciples asked when God's kingdom would begin and what the warning signs would be. The warning signs are the events of the seven-year Tribulation. The Millennial Kingdom will begin immediately after the Tribulation period, when Christ returns to the earth with power and glory. The Church will be with Him, and angels will gather all the believers on earth to begin His earthly kingdom. When trees put out their leaves, we know that summer is near. Likewise, when all these things happen, we know the Millennial Kingdom is near. God alone knows the exact day and hour it begins. As earthly servants should always be ready for their master's return, the servants of God should be ready.

As Christians, we are waiting for the Rapture. Are you watchful and ready, confessing your sin? Are you serving faithfully until He comes?

Monday · MARK 14:1-11

Q

A

DIGGING DEEPER · Many times the villain in a story is someone unexpected. As usual, the religious leaders were plotting to kill Jesus, yet they were afraid of riots by the large Passover crowd. Passover celebrates the death angel "passing over" the Israelites while killing the firstborn of every Egyptian household–the event which caused Pharaoh to let the Israelites go. A woman poured a bottle of a very ex-pensive perfume on Jesus because she loved Him. Some complained that the money from the perfume should be given to poor people. Jesus, knowing He would die soon, told them she was preparing His body for burial. The unexpected villain was one of His disciples, though Jesus knew all along (John 6:70-71).

What are you willing to give Jesus out of love? How much will you sacrifice? We should put worshiping God ahead of serving others. Do you?

Tuesday · MARK 14:12-21

Q

A

DIGGING DEEPER · On the first Passover, everyone who killed a lamb and spread its blood over their door was spared by the death angel. Jesus is our Passover lamb, and His blood spread over our sin spares us from eternal death in Hell. It was not an accident that Jesus was crucified during Passover. Everything was happening according to God's plan. As they ate supper, Jesus predicted one of the twelve would betray Him. Every disciple questioned whether it would be him. Not one pointed a finger at Judas. He did not stand out as someone faking belief in Christ. The things happening to Jesus were just as the prophets had written—even Judas' betrayal. Yet that was no excuse for Judas, and his punishment was severe.

It is difficult to identify false Christians. Are you a true believer? Have you allowed Jesus' blood to wash over your sins by placing your faith in Him?

Wednesday · MARK 14:22-31

Q

A

DIGGING DEEPER • Certain foods often remind us of things. Jesus gave the disciples and all who came after them a reminder of His sacrifice in the bread and wine of the Passover feast. The bread reminds us of His body, which was beaten and nailed to a cross for our benefit. The wine reminds us of His blood, which was shed to cover the sins of all believers throughout history. Today, this remembering of Jesus' sacrifice is called the Lord's Supper. Later, Jesus prophesied that all His disciples would run away scared when He was arrested. Peter objected, and Jesus prophesied he would deny knowing Him three times before morning.
How seriously do you take the Lord's Supper? What do you think about during the Lord's Supper? Do you deny Jesus in difficult situations?

Thursday · MARK 14:32-42

Q

A

DIGGING DEEPER • Sometimes the dread of a difficult task can be overwhelming. Thinking of the betrayal, trial, mockery, beating, and death He was about to experience, Jesus became overwhelmed and sad. As a result, He took His three closest followers with Him to pray. Instead of praying with Him, Peter, James, and John fell asleep. This was the most difficult time of Jesus' life, and His closest followers showed no awareness of His need for their prayers. Finding them asleep, Jesus told them to be alert and pray so they could resist falling into temptation. They wanted to do the right thing but had not learned how easy it was to neglect prayer. Prayer is an excellent weapon against sin and temptation.
Are you willing to do God's will even when it is difficult? Do you pray and seek others' prayer during difficult times? How do you resist temptation?

Friday · MARK 14:43-52

Q
A

DIGGING DEEPER • A kiss is usually an act of love and respect. Yet, Judas betrayed Jesus with a kiss. While pretending to show love and respect, Judas showed the soldiers whom to arrest. Even though Jesus taught publicly in the temple every day, the religious leaders sent a large group of armed men to arrest Him in the night like a criminal in hiding. From the Gospel of John, we learn that it was Peter who cut the ear off one man. Jesus put it back on, according to the Gospel of Luke. Afterward all the disciples ran away in fear. The young man who lost his clothes is a bit of a mystery. Many believe it was Mark, the writer of this Gospel. Perhaps it was included to show that he, too, was fearful and ran away like all the rest.

Is your love and respect for Christ sincere? Is there a price for which you would betray Jesus? Are you afraid to stand with Jesus?

Saturday · MARK 14:53-65

Q
A

DIGGING DEEPER • Jesus was brought before a corrupt court of religious leaders. Peter followed at a distance and came close enough to see what was happening. He did not stand by Jesus like he promised, but was much closer than the other disciples. During the trial, several false witnesses testified against Jesus, but they could not get their lies straight. They twisted Jesus' words and contradicted each other. Just as was prophesied, Jesus did not say one word in His own defense. Frustrated, the high priest asked Him directly if He was Christ, the Son of God. He said "yes," so the high priest accused Him of blasphemy—wrongly claiming rights and power that belong only to God. Of course, he was wrong, because Jesus is God.

Do you courageously stand up for Jesus or lurk in the shadows, hoping not to be seen? How do you show belief that Jesus is Christ, the Son of God?

QuietTime

WEEK 17

In this week's passage you will find the greatest event in history. The most significant accomplishments of men cannot compare. No scientist, doctor, musician, king, president, general, or religious leader has ever done anything that can rival Jesus' accomplishment in this passage.

Prayer focus for this week

THE QUESTION *What is the writer saying?*
THE ANSWER *How Can I apply this to my life?*

Sunday · MARK 14:66-72

DIGGING DEEPER • There are few feelings worse than the guilt and embarrassment of failure. When the servant girl recognized Peter, he lied and denied knowing Jesus. Peter was accused twice more, and denied Jesus two more times. The third time, he cursed and swore to convince them. The swearing was an oath similar to swearing to tell the truth in court. After the rooster crowed, Jesus looked at Peter (Luke 22:61). That look must have been devastating. Peter remembered that he had told Jesus that he would never forsake Him and then that was what he had just done. This guilt caused him to weep.

Have you ever been accused of being a Christian? If so, how did you react? If not, why? When was the last time you wept over your sin?

Monday · MARK 15:1-15

Q

A

DIGGING DEEPER · The religious leaders broke their own law by having Jesus' trial at night. The next morning they met again to make the guilty verdict official. They could not execute prisoners, so they took Him to the Roman Governor, Pilate. He realized that Jesus was innocent and that the religious leaders were motivated by jealousy. It was a custom for Pilate to release a prisoner during the Passover feast. He thought the people would choose Jesus. Instead, the multitude asked for Barabbas, a murderer, to be released and for Jesus to die in his place. It was a decision that Pilate would live to regret.

Are you thankful Jesus died in your place? Have you thought about the suffering Jesus went through? How does this affect your lifestyle?

Tuesday · MARK 15:16-26

Q

A

DIGGING DEEPER · Jesus was taken to the Praetorium, or official residence of the Governor of Jerusalem. The whole garrison, consisting of six hundred men, gathered to mock Him. Since He was claiming to be the King of the Jews, they dressed Him in the royal color purple, put a crown of thorns on His head, and saluted Him. In mock reverence, they bowed and worshiped Him. Severely wounded by beating and flogging, He was unable to carry the heavy crossbeam to His crucifixion. A man named Simon was ordered to carry it for Him. Jesus refused a mixture of wine and myrrh intended to dull the pain and make nailing Him to the cross easier. Soldiers gambled for His clothes, fulfilling prophecy (Psalm 22:18).

What does the severity of Christ's suffering cause you to think? Are you willing to serve others even if it means suffering and great difficulty?

Wednesday · MARK 15:27-38

DIGGING DEEPER · The cross of Christ appears to be a tragedy. Yet, it is the greatest victory ever won—the victory over sin. At noon, it became dark for three hours. During this time, Jesus bore our sins and the wrath of God for those sins. When He cried out, "My God, my God, why hast thou forsaken me?" it was because He had be-come sin for us. Christ's worst suffering was not the physical pain. It was bearing God's wrath and being forsaken for our sins. The veil in the temple separated the Holy Place from the Holy of Holies. It separated a holy God from sinful man. When Jesus died, the veil was torn from top to bottom. The separation between God and man was removed. We now have access to God through Jesus Christ.
Do you understand that Jesus suffered God's wrath on the cross for your sins? Have you trusted completely in the cross of Christ for salvation?

Thursday · MARK 15:39-47

DIGGING DEEPER · The centurion at the foot of the cross heard Jesus yell out and then breathe His final breath. Based on this, he was convinced that Jesus was the Son of God. When Joseph of Arimathea went to Pilate and requested the body, Pilate was surprised that Jesus was already dead. He checked with the centurion to verify the death. Why were Pilate and the centurion so impressed by Jesus' death? History indicates that victims of crucifixion normally die from suffocation and can linger for days. The centurion was impressed because a suffocating man should not be able to yell. Pilate was impressed because He died in just six hours. The point is that Jesus laid down His life for us; it was not taken from Him.
Jesus gave His life for you. What will you give to Him? Some were not afraid to be associated with Christ. Are you?

Friday · MARK 16:1-8

Q

A

DIGGING DEEPER • Jewish tradition was to anoint or rub spices on dead bodies to cover the smell of decay. Some women came to anoint Jesus on Sunday morning. This was the third day after Jesus' death, and they expected Him to be in the tomb. Obviously, they did not understand or believe His prophesy of rising from the dead on the third day. The disciples did not believe it, either, because they were nowhere to be found. When the women arrived at the tomb, an angel told them Jesus had risen from the dead. He sent word for the disciples and Peter to meet Jesus in Galilee as planned. Even though Peter had flatly denied Him three times, Jesus was still eager to see him. Even when we fail, Jesus is gracious and forgiving.
Do you believe Jesus will do what He says? If so, how have you shown that lately? Are you avoiding the gracious Savior because of sin?

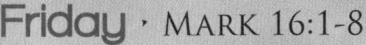

Saturday · MARK 16:9-20

Q

A

DIGGING DEEPER • As mentioned previously, the disciples did not believe Jesus would rise from the dead. They even refused to believe when eyewitnesses saw the resurrected Lord. They did not believe until Jesus personally appeared to them and rebuked them for their hard hearts. He then commanded them to preach the Gospel to the world. The signs mentioned in vv. 17-18 were only for the early church. They validated the message of the disciples, just as Jesus' miracles validated His message. Jesus then ascended up to Heaven and took His rightful place of honor by God, the Father. Everywhere the disciples preached, the Lord worked through them and validated what they taught with miraculous signs.
What does it take to get you to believe what the Bible teaches? Is your heart hard, or soft and open to the Word? Are you preaching the Gospel?

QuietTime

WEEK 18

If there's ever a passage of Scripture you don't want to miss, this is it! Are you really walking with Christ each day? What do you do if you're not? How do you keep yourself walking with Him? How do you know your friends are walking with Him? No matter how old you are, this week is crucial! Dive in with all you've got!

Prayer focus for this week

THE QUESTION THE ANSWER

What is the writer saying?
How Can I apply this to my life?

Sunday · 1 JOHN 1:1-4

Q

A

DIGGING DEEPER • Ever wonder if you're really walking with Christ? Are you living the Christian life like God wants you to? Just about every believer wonders at some point. John tells us that this is actually why he wrote this book. You can have fellowship with Christ, and you can be certain about it. Who would know better about a friendship with Christ than someone who saw Him, touched Him, and walked with Him for three years on earth? That was John. We also know from Scripture that no one was closer with Christ than John. John lets us know there is awesome joy in walking with Christ. What a thought! John wants us to know that we can have a personal relationship with the very Son of God daily.

Do you have awesome joy in your relationship with Christ? Are you going to be committed to learning about walking in fellowship with Him?

Monday · 1 JOHN 1:5-10

Q

A

DIGGING DEEPER · How does a Christian handle sin? That is the first basic topic John talks about. When it comes to walking with Christ day by day, sin gets in the way. First of all, you can't ignore it. Verse 6 says we lie when we don't admit our own sin. Everybody sins now and then-just admit it to God! He knows when we blow it, and so do we. The only way to walk with Christ day by day is to keep sin out of our life. So how do you do that? Verse 9! You need to admit it to God, and focus on not doing it again. He will cleanse you so that you are back in a right relationship with Him. Tolerating sin in our lives as Christians is really a lousy place to be. Yes, we still sin as Christians, but we can make it right any time!
Is there any sin in your life you have not admitted or confessed to God? Why not confess it? What are you going to do to stay away from it?

Tuesday · 1 JOHN 2:1-6

Q

A

DIGGING DEEPER · Now that we know there is a way to take care of our sin, it doesn't mean we do what we want, and just confess it later. John's point in writing was so that we *wouldn't sin* (v. 1). Just in case you don't feel forgiven, remember Who speaks on your behalf: Jesus Christ Himself (v. 2)! If we sin, does it mean we're not saved? Verses 3-6 give us the key. There ought to be a desire to obey God's Word. He knows we're not perfect. That's why John wrote chapter 1. A genuine Christian will be working on pursuing Christ more than anything else. Check out your life. Christ doesn't need lawyers; He's our advocate (lawyer). What He wants are witnesses. In this case, it's both what we do and say that counts.
Do you truly have a desire to follow Christ? Is it great enough to cause you to obey God's Word instead of doing what you want?

Wednesday · 1 JOHN 2:7-11

DIGGING DEEPER · So what's up with the "old" and "new" command? The command to love each other isn't new. These Christians in 1 John knew that. What was new about it was *doing* it through *Christ*. They now knew what perfect love was because Christ's death showed it to everyone (2:2). Verses 9-11 give one of those commands John was talking about in verse 3: you can't walk with Christ and not love other believers. Verse 11 gives some insight to a Christian who doesn't love: you are blind! You may think your friendship with God is OK, but it's not! You have to be in tune with God *and* all your fellow Christians. It's not just about whether you "hate" them. The question is, are you busy loving them?

Do you have a conflict with other Christians? Are you being honest with yourself? How are you going to show love to them?

Thursday · 1 JOHN 2:12-17

DIGGING DEEPER · Verses 12-14 identify three different levels of Christians: "little children"—recently saved; "young men"—those saved for awhile and moving on to spiritual maturity; and "fathers"—those aged and mature Christians who have come through the *little children* and *young men* stage. John uses these levels to remind the people that not every believer is at the same place in his Christian walk. It takes time to grow in the things John is telling them about, like in verses 15-17. Another command follows. "The world" refers to society and its culture of pleasure, materialism, and popularity. You can't love that stuff! Love is for people and God, not for society.

What in this world are you tempted to love? What are you going to do to stay away from it? Do you love doing God's will more than anything else?

Friday · 1 JOHN 2:18-22

Q

A

DIGGING DEEPER · Lots of people call themselves Christians. We don't have to point the finger and judge them, but we can tell the difference. There is the antichrist of Revelation 13:1-10, but John is referring to those who weren't saved and were stirring up trouble in the church. They were a group of people pretending to be Christians, but they eventually left the church. John uses them as examples of those who don't follow Christ's commands (v. 3), don't love fellow Christians (v. 9), but are in love with the world (v. 15). As genuine Christians, we have the Holy Spirit living inside of us, and He helps us discern between truth and error. Be careful about those with whom you fellowship.
Are you really close friends with those who may not be saved? Have you graciously talked to them about Jesus? Are you truly following Christ?

Saturday · 1 JOHN 2:23-27

Q

A

DIGGING DEEPER · We learn here that it is critical what you believe about Jesus. There are many ideas about who Jesus was and what He did, but it is vital to believe exactly what the Bible says about Him. The number one reason is that you can't be saved unless you believe Jesus is God. The basic truths of Christ are also important for how we live. We need to know more about Jesus each day, because it affects how we handle sin, how we love each other, and whether or not we love the world. John wrote this because there were people who were teaching false things about Jesus. Verse 24 tells us that's another way you know whether you're really walking with God! Staying in fellowship with the Lord also keeps us from sin.
What are you doing to learn more about Christ? What are you going to do to know Christ better? Who could help you know Christ better?

QuietTime

WEEK 19

This week could be summed up in one word—love. There are many different ways His love should influence us. That includes our relationships with others and with God, and His relationship to others. If you get a handle on His love, then you are guaranteed to truly walk with the Lord like never before!

Prayer focus for this week

THE QUESTION · *What is the writer saying?*
THE ANSWER · *How Can I apply this to my life?*

Sunday · 1 JOHN 2:28-3:3

DIGGING DEEPER • John finishes up chapter 2 with a summary statement—a challenge. You will know that you and others are walking in fellowship with God because your lifestyle and deeds will show it. End of story. John now turns to a deeper subject. He moves from "fellowship" to "sonship." What a privilege! That's amazing! When we see Him, we will be like Him. Knowing that should cause two things. We should look forward to an amazing future with the Father. Also, as we wait for Him, we need to be ready at any moment for His coming. We need to be a child in whom the Father will be well pleased when He comes. No matter what your past has been, your future can be spotless.

If Christ returned at this very second, would He be pleased with your life? What can you do to honor Him? What should you stop doing?

Monday · 1 JOHN 3:4-10

Q
A

DIGGING DEEPER • John is using the logic that people who please God are the children of God, and people who constantly sin are not the children of God. So what if the same sin keeps tripping you up? Does that mean you're not a child of God? Not necessarily. John does clarify that a genuine Christian does not *continue in sin*. Someone who really knows Christ will eventually turn around. The question for us is this: "does my life characterize sin...or godly living?" False teachers in this church were unmistakably characterized by sinful, selfish living. John just says, "Look at their life." We don't decide who is saved and who isn't, but we do know how to spot someone who loves God versus someone who loves this world.

What would your parents, brothers, or sisters say about you? Do people think of you as a godly Christian, or as just another person?

Tuesday · 1 JOHN 3:11-16

Q
A

DIGGING DEEPER • So how much of your life should be characterized by godly living? How much good is good enough? Our actions ought to be very easy to recognize. John uses the example of Cain and Abel. Cain hated his brother because his brother's life was characterized by godliness. Even if Abel was a more mature believer, Cain should never have hated him, let alone killed him. John comes back to loving each other. So, how do you know if you really love others? Verse 16 asks if you are willing to serve and do anything, even die for another believer. As Christians, we really should stand out. Consider this: your love for God is only as great as the Christian you like the least. You may want to read that statement a few times.

What Christians do you have the hardest time loving? What are you going to do to show love to them?

Wednesday · 1 JOHN 3:17-24

DIGGING DEEPER • Do you ever question whether or not you are saved? Do you ever feel like you're not saved? Do you ever feel like God isn't listening when you pray? As believers, we should have a clear conscience when it comes to loving one another. If verses 21-23 are true of you, how you *feel* doesn't determine whether or not you're a child of God! If our hearts condemn us (we don't feel saved), we can still be at peace. God is greater than how we feel! Salvation is based on believing in Christ and having the Spirit of God living in us (v. 23). The evidence of our living godly lives will also follow. Assurance of our salvation comes from what God says is true of a Christian, not from how you feel!

Do you base your salvation on your feelings or on the truth of God's Word? What should you remember the next time you don't feel saved?

Thursday · 1 JOHN 4:1-6

DIGGING DEEPER • There are many ideas today that describe how to get to Heaven and Who Jesus is. We hear preachers, schoolteachers, TV, and a host of other sources all the time. How do you know who is teaching right from wrong? That's what "test" or *try the spirits* means. 2 Peter 1:21 teaches that the Spirit of God wrote the Bible through men. The way you know whether someone is telling the truth is whether what they say and do agrees with the Bible. That even includes your pastor or Sunday School teacher! Does it line up with all that the Bible says? Sound scary or hard? Remember verse 4! God is greater than anything Satan could try to confuse us with. We've got His perfect Word! It's never wrong!

Have you ever questioned something someone was teaching you? Did you go check it out in the Bible? Who can help you understand God's Word?

Friday · 1 JOHN 4:7-12

Q

A

DIGGING DEEPER •   So what is *real* love, according to the Bible? Not a *love* for pizza, or a *love* for your clothes. This whole passage is a great definition. There's only one way to know true love. You have to be born of God first—become a Christian. Real love comes from God. It started with Him, and He's the only one Who can help you love like He did. It's impossible to manifest this love on your own! The best example of real love is verse 9. Verse 9 is almost an echo of John 3:16. No wonder! The same person who wrote John 3:16 wrote this book also! The word *propitiation*, or substitute, is the most important word in verse 10. If we want to really love others, then we've got to better understand Christ's love for us. If you really want to love, everybody else has to come before yourself!
Do you consider yourself better than others? How can you put others first?

Saturday · 1 JOHN 4:13-21

Q

A

DIGGING DEEPER •   Love is a very important attribute of God, and also very important in the walk of the believer. In fact, without God's love to us, and our returned love to Him, it would be impossible to live like He wants us to. Our love for Him is the only true motivation for why we do what we do. That's how *love is perfected in us*. For example, we can be afraid of many things, but there really is no reason to fear anything. Why? We have been made secure in Christ by God's love. We can't lose His love, nor will He ever take it away. God loves us too much to purposely harm us without a reason. Even when difficult things happen, God's love allows them to make us more like Him. He also makes it possible for us to love others.
What is it that you are afraid of? How should God's love for you take that fear away? What friend in Christ could you show love to today?

QuietTime

WEEK 20

John had a great love for the people to whom he was writing. As we finish 1 John and move to 2 and 3 John, we will see that the letters were addressed to different people. All sorts of difficult problems are addressed, but they are the same problems we deal with all the time. These are short but powerful letters!

Prayer focus for this week

THE QUESTION · *What is the writer saying?*
THE ANSWER · *How Can I apply this to my life?*

Sunday · 1 JOHN 5:1-8

DIGGING DEEPER · John continues his three main thoughts: loving God, loving fellow believers, and obeying God's commands. All three must be true of us. If we are neglecting any one of them, we are disobeying the other two as well. They are all connected. This is how we walk with God. John goes one step further, though. This is also how we overcome the world. We have challenges, hard times, bullies, and all sorts of obstacles to deal with. Here's the key! Here's how we overcome them! We just walk with God, stay in fellowship with Him each day, and confess our sins. That doesn't solve all our problems, but if we focus on our relationship with Christ first, He will take care of the rest. That's how we overcome the world!

What is difficult in your life right now? Will you give it to the Lord, and just focus on walking with Him today? Will you commit to not worrying?

Monday · 1 JOHN 5:9-15

Q

A

DIGGING DEEPER · Ever feel you can't do anything right? Maybe you lack confidence in sports, music, school, or work? God wants you to have confidence, but He wants you to have confidence and faith in Him first (v. 13). Secondly, when you pray, you can have complete confidence that He hears you! The key is this: when you pray and ask the Lord for specific requests, you pray "according to His will," *and* are willing to submit to whatever He decides for you. The confidence we have is knowing that He wants to bless us, and He's going to give us exactly what we need. The bottom line is that we can trust the Lord in everything!

What situation do you need to pray about right now? Are you willing to submit to God's answer for you?

Tuesday · 1 JOHN 5:16-21

Q

A

DIGGING DEEPER · Verses 16-17 speak of two sins, one of which leads to physical death. The sin that leads to death refers to a Christian who repeatedly sins without remorse and has gone too far in his sin, at which time God decides to take him home. That's one reason a Christian cannot continue in sin. God will eventually call him home! The other reference is to a Christian brother praying for another Christian who has sinned. This should be a prayer for the sinner's repentance and confession (1 John 1:9). The last sentence in the book is awesome! John's point was to make sure nothing in our lives would come before our relationship with Christ. Anything can take the place of our Lord. We need to see that nothing does!

Is there a sinning brother or sister in Christ for whom you should be praying? Is there sin in your life that you need to confess to God?

Wednesday · 2 John 1-6

DIGGING DEEPER • The "lady" in this book is most likely a person who had a church meeting in her house. John knew her and had great joy to see her particular children obeying God. This letter was probably addressed to a different church than in 1 John. That's why John starts off talking about the same things he did in the previous book: that we should love one another and obey God's Word. John is actually doing the very thing he told them to do. By writing this letter to this specific lady, he's showing how much he cared for her and her children. John was concerned about the Christians in that area and he had a warning to give them. He was clearly thinking of others instead of himself.

To what Christian friend could you reach out today? What is the best way for you to be an encouragement to him?

Thursday · 2 John 7-12

Q

A

DIGGING DEEPER • This lady had teachers come into her home to teach the other believers there. John needed to warn her about the false teachers who were in that area. He warned her about letting them into her home. She needed to stay away from them. False teaching is very dangerous. It is critical for us to surround ourselves with friends and people who love Christ. There are many religions out there, but only one true God, one Jesus, and one way to Heaven. We need to fully submerge ourselves in His Word in order to stay away from some of the wrong teaching that is out there today.

How are you doing at studying God's Word and learning about Christ? Do you blindly agree with anyone who talks about God, or do you graciously stand up for Jesus and His Word?

Friday · 3 JOHN 1-8

Q

A

DIGGING DEEPER • Gaius was a special friend to John. Gaius may have spent lots of time with John. Gaius was faithful in a church where a bad guy was stirring up trouble. There were some faithful brothers coming to this church, and "Mr. Bad Guy" wouldn't welcome them. Gaius took care of them, and made sure they had a place to stay and food to eat. The problem was that Gaius loved God, but "Mr. Bad Guy" loved himself. They were both leaders in the church. Gaius needed to stand firm for the faithful brothers, and it probably was hard for him and made him unpopular. Gaius could have just gotten along with everyone. Instead, he went further by welcoming the faithful brothers, and pleasing God instead of pleasing people.

What Christian around you is unpopular or made fun of? How can you reach out to him, even if it makes you seem unpopular?

Saturday · 3 JOHN 9-14

Q

A

DIGGING DEEPER • The "Mr. Bad Guy" of this passage is named Diotrephes. So how bad was he? He always wanted to be first. He spread bad rumors about the Apostle John. He kicked out the faithful brothers whom John had sent, as well as those who disagreed with him. That's what Gaius had to deal with. John reminded Gaius not to be frustrated or to try to fight Diotrephes—not to do the same thing Diotrephes was doing, causing a power struggle in the church. John was coming to the church shortly, and he would handle it. The important thing was not to be nasty like Diotrophes. It's easy to think it's fair to return evil for evil, but John encouraged Gaius to always do good.

Have you recently done something that was wrong, because someone did it to you? Are your words gracious, even when people speak badly of you?

QuietTime

WEEK 21

How would you feel if you were kidnapped and then, 10 years later, you got to go home? This week we will see how God rescued the Israelites after they had been away from home for 70 years. We will see how some people will try to discourage God's work. The big truth this week is that God is always in control.

Prayer focus for this week

THE QUESTION
THE ANSWER

What is the writer saying?
How Can I apply this to my life?

Sunday · EZRA 1:1-11

DIGGING DEEPER · Here we read of an historical event that demonstrates that even when God punishes us, His ultimate plan is to bring us back into true worship. After 70 years of bondage, God put in King Cyrus's heart to let the Jews go home, and to give them money, food, and supplies to get there. In order for the people to truly worship, they needed their temple rebuilt. The king helped pay for the rebuilding, and returned some articles that had been stolen. We see here how God can choose to use pagan people to accomplish His purpose for our lives. The King of Babylon was still under the sovereign rule of the God of Heaven. The phrase *God of Heaven* is used nine times in the book of Ezra.

What does it take to get you to be obedient to God? Do you find comfort in knowing God is in control? God loves you and wants you to worship Him.

Monday · EZRA 2:1, 64-70

Q

A

DIGGING DEEPER · This is the record of those who returned to Jerusalem and Judah, adding up to about 50,000 people. When God rescued the Israelites from Pharaoh, the ruler of Egypt, around 1445 B.C., there were an estimated two million people who followed Moses. About 1,000 years later, only about 2.5% of these made the trip back home to rebuild the temple. These few fully devoted believers in Jehovah God gave sacrificially for the privilege of having a place to worship. It had been 70 years since they had been able to be home to worship like they wanted to. **It's been around 2,000 years since Jesus died on the cross. What would you be willing to sacrifice in order to be able to serve Him? Show the Lord how grateful you are for a place to worship by doing a Christian Service at church.**

Tuesday · EZRA 3:1-13

Q

A

DIGGING DEEPER · We can't imagine the excitement and joy that was going on at this great reunion. As soon as the Jews were geographically in a position to worship, they began to prepare their hearts spiritually. The purpose of the sacrificial system of worship was to develop a sensitive heart toward sin. God said that without the shedding of blood there was no forgiveness of sin (Hebrews 9:22). Sacrificing an animal demonstrated repentance of sin and obedience to God. After about two years of collecting material and money for the temple, the Jews began to break ground. It had been around 50 years since Solomon's Temple was destroyed; therefore, there was weeping over memories and shouts of joy for the future temple. **Do you know that Jesus is our blood sacrifice? Are you excited about going to church and learning about God and His Word?**

Wednesday · EZRA 4:1-5

Q

A

DIGGING DEEPER · Here we see that nothing has changed in over 2500 years. When you want to do something or build something for God, the Evil One will use his people to try to discourage and destroy the whole project. The Jews were ready to build. Some other people who didn't serve the same God acted like they wanted to help, but their true motive was to be a hindrance to God's work. The leaders realized they were liars and told them that they couldn't help. Then their true character was exposed, and they lied and deceived the king who had originally told them to build. The building of the temple was slowed down for about 15 years.
If you're in a church that's trying to go forward for God and grow, do you help out, or are you a hindrance? Do you say or do things that do not honor God, just so you can have your way?

Thursday · EZRA 4:6-16

Q

A

DIGGING DEEPER · The people that got mad at the Jews were not going to rest until they fulfilled Satan's goals. These people who were against the building of the temple were not even best friends, but they had a common enemy called the Jews, God's chosen people. Therefore, it was easy to get people who had a common enemy (Jews) to write a letter to the king, warning him about these people—saying they were rebuilding to revolt. The letter was intended to raise concern in two areas: one was power, and the other was greed. It's never difficult to find those who want to hinder the work of God. They are willing to risk a great deal to accomplish their task. Perhaps we can take a positive lesson from them.
Try to remember that people who do not love Jesus probably will not like you, either. Even when your circumstances look bad, God is in control.

Friday · EZRA 4:17-24

Q

A

DIGGING DEEPER • The king reacted very quickly to the letter and sent a reply back to the enemies of the Jews, allowing them to stop the Jews from rebuilding. Needless to say, he never allowed them to finish the work. It wasn't until a new king came into power that construction began again. If the people (the Jews) had known how much hassle their sin was going to cause them, they probably wouldn't have rebelled against God. God has a way of allowing us to go through trials to test our loyalty to Him. The hottest fire only separates the dross from the pure metal!

Have you ever disobeyed God and wished you hadn't? How long does it take for you to repent and turn back to God? "Trust and obey, for there's no other way to be happy in Jesus, but to trust and obey."

Saturday · EZRA 5:1-5

Q

A

DIGGING DEEPER • God doesn't just sit by and let His people not hear from Him. The Lord began to speak to the men of God called prophets, and told them to tell the people it was time to start building again. So the people and the prophets got busy for God. Then the men in charge of protecting that area showed up and asked why the Jews had started building again. God's people didn't have anything to hide. They gave Tatnai all the information he needed. They had learned that God is faithful and that He would be with them. Once the Lord places something on your heart to do for Him, even if it's changing jobs, moving, picking new friends, breaking up, or whatever; you don't lean on your own understanding...but on God's.

If God wanted you to step out in faith and do something you were uncomfortable with, would you trust God enough to do it?

QuietTime

WEEK 22

Have you ever been in a situation where you were scared to do what was right because you thought that you would get in trouble, or that it would cost you? This week we will see how doing it God's way is the only way. Ezra was a man doing it God's way by faith, trust, and obedience. This is a big GOD week.

Prayer focus for this week

THE QUESTION · *What is the writer saying?*
THE ANSWER · *How Can I apply this to my life?*

Sunday · EZRA 5:6-17

DIGGING DEEPER · Here is the response of the government official to King Darius. As we read, we see that the people of God cooperated with the government, giving them the information they needed. The Bible says we are to obey the laws of the land, and that God Himself has established the government for our good. When you have nothing to hide, you can use life's circumstances to give a testimony of the God you serve. Both in their words and countenance, the Jews showed faithfulness to their God and to the government without compromising Scripture. Ephesians 5:15-16 says we are to be careful how we walk, not as unwise men but wise, using our time wisely because the days are evil. (See also Colossians 4:5)

How does it affect our testimony when we disobey the law and try to out smart the government? Are you abstaining from the appearance of evil?

Monday · EZRA 6:1-12

Q

A

DIGGING DEEPER • This is an awesome testimony of how God is in control. King Darius read the letter from King Cyrus giving permission to the Jews to begin the rebuilding of the temple, and ordering that their gold and silver utensils be returned to the temple. At this time, King Darius ordered his people to leave the Jews alone and let them continue building. Not only was he allowing the Jews to build, but he was going to take money from the royal treasury and help them pay for it. That's not all… King Darius also gave them anything they needed to worship their God. Then he said that anyone who tried to stop the Jews would lose his own house. God shows His people again that the heart of the king is in His hand.
Can you see why it's better to do right and trust God? Is there anything that you need to trust God with right now? Our God reigns!

Tuesday · EZRA 6:13-22

Q

A

DIGGING DEEPER • The temple being completed is the result of God being in control. When the people of God follow the leaders that God has established, the results will bring glory to the Lord. A sign of God getting the glory is the people demonstrating repentance, sacrifice, and purity. The goodness of God draws men to repentance. The people were also preparing their hearts and lives to celebrate the Passover, a ceremony in memory of being set free from the bondage of Egypt. The Israelites had truly come to a place of worshiping Jehovah God again and it was evident by the purity of their homes, personal lives, and ministers.
Have you ever experienced true repentance to the point of sacrifice and purity? Are you willing to separate yourself unto God and give back to God His glory in your life? What should you lay on the altar today?

Wednesday · EZRA 7:1-10

Q

A

DIGGING DEEPER · Nearly 60 years have gone by, and the Israelites are struggling with their walk again. God is never surprised about the sin of people; neither is He unprepared to deal with it. God had a man whom He was preparing privately for a public ministry. The reason for telling the heritage of Ezra was to let the people know he was from a godly family, and qualified to give an answer of hope to them. Ezra knew he couldn't do it by himself, so he took others with him to help with the journey and ministry. Ezra was known as a man whose heart was set on God and His Word, and who taught biblical principles that he himself had applied. That's why it's repeated six times that *the good hand of the Lord was upon him*.

Isn't it good to know that God is preparing us now for future ministry? Which area of Christian Service could you do this weekend? Do it.

Thursday · EZRA 7:11-28

Q

A

DIGGING DEEPER · This has got to be one of the best examples of God controlling the affairs of His people and demonstrating His control over the hearts of kings (Proverbs 21:1). Here we see God honoring the faithfulness of His servant Ezra and giving him above and beyond all that he could ask or think. It's also a testimony of God meeting the needs of people who don't know that He is preparing people and provisions for a future need or work project. As you look at what God did for Israel through the man of God, Ezra, stop and ask God to use you to bring people back to the Lord for worship and service. Ezra was a man of integrity and was known to do the Lord's will.

Is God blessing your life and ministry more than you could ask or think? Do you have a good testimony with your unsaved friends?

Friday · EZRA 8:1, 15-23

Q

A

DIGGING DEEPER • The journey to Jerusalem begins for Ezra and about three to four thousand others. Ezra was concerned about the spiritual needs of the people, but when he realized that he didn't have any Levites with him to teach the Law and maintain discipline in the temple, he instructed some men in recruiting the Levites for this trip. Because Ezra knew that God had His hand on him, he wanted himself and the people to remain humble. So he called the people together to fast and pray that God would protect them and their possessions as they traveled. Ezra could have asked for help from the local government, but he didn't; he taught his people to trust God. God answered their prayers and protected them.
Is God more concerned about our relationship with Him, or what we do for Him? Is there anything in your life for which God isn't getting the glory?

Saturday · EZRA 8:24-36

Q

A

DIGGING DEEPER • Ezra committed to 12 priests of the tribe of Levi the task of moving 25+ tons of gold and silver, as the priests were the only ones allowed to handle the treasure. This trip was several hundred miles and took several months. The priests' responsibility was to protect the treasure until every ounce was accounted for upon arrival in Jerusalem. After a few days of rest, it was time to reconcile with the accountants, and all was accounted for (2 Corinthians 8:21). From this point on, it was all about worship. Psalm 122:1-2 says, *I was glad when they said unto me, Let us go into the house of the Lord. Our feet shall stand within thy gates, O Jerusalem.* Ezra truly had the good hand of God on his life and this journey.
Isn't it good to know that when God is for you, no one can be against you? We serve a BIG God who wants to use us for His glory. Just trust Him!

QuietTime

WEEK 23

How do you feel when you do a favor for someone and they don't say thank you or even act like they know you? This week we will see how Ezra was upset at the ungrateful people. He was so upset that he pulled out his hair and went without food. We will also see how God feels about helping ministries with money.

Prayer focus for this week

THE QUESTION *What is the writer saying?*
THE ANSWER *How Can I apply this to my life?*

Sunday · EZRA 9:1-5

DIGGING DEEPER · Ezra had now been back in Jerusalem for about four months, and his worst nightmare was about to unfold before his eyes. Some of Ezra's friends who had the same good value system told him that there was a lot of sin in the camp. With no fear of God, the people and the religious leaders were marrying with and following in the idolatrous ways of the heathen nations all around them. Ezra was so upset that he tore his clothes, pulled out his own hair, and sat down and wept. At about 3 o'clock, when they begin their sacrificial system, Ezra was there to beg God for mercy for the people. While he was seeking God's face, the people who feared the God of Israel gathered around him and prayed with him.

How do you respond to the sin of your country, your work place, or school? When you sin, does it grieve you? Do you have a holy fear of God?

Monday · EZRA 9: 6-15

Q

A

DIGGING DEEPER • Ezra is a spiritually broken man before God. He knows that the sin of a few is seen as the sin of the nation. These mixed marriages were sin. Ezra begins his prayer with humility and responsibility, as a spiritual leader bearing the burden of his people's sin. He shares his heart about the sin of the past, and how God had punished the nation for their rebellion. Then Ezra shows a grateful spirit for the undeserved blessings of deliverance from slavery and God's working in the king's heart to help rebuild the temple. He then says that his people are without excuse. Even after God's punishment, they have continued to rebel against His Word. If they get what they deserve, none of them will survive.
Don't ever forget what God has done and is doing for you. Do you show a grateful spirit to Jesus by living a life that is applying His Word?

Tuesday · EZRA 10:1-9

Q

A

DIGGING DEEPER • Ezra drew a crowd by weeping, praying, and confessing in front of the temple. God answered his prayer through Shechaniah, who represented the people and confessed their sin against God. Not only did he confess, but he also was willing to make an oath to God to get rid of the heathen women and children, and to keep the commandments of God. Ezra called for a meeting with all the people, to confess and get right with God. Those who didn't would be punished. Ezra never lost focus on the importance of fasting, prayer, and being broken before God. He was now ready to go and preach repentance to the people.
Do you believe that God honors sacrificial praying? Have you ever wept before God in broken repentance? How does your sin affect others?

Wednesday · EZRA 10:10-19, 44

DIGGING DEEPER • After much counsel and communion with God, Ezra preached to the people about their sin against God that had caused Israel to be put in a position of bondage and punishment. He demanded confession of sin and separation from it. All the people obeyed, and the process started. Every person who had married a non-Israelite was brought up before the judges and elders of the city, who decided what to do. This process took approximately three months. There were a few who disagreed, but the cleansing of sin continued. Public rebellion required public repentance; therefore, the priest's names are recorded forever in Scripture for sinning against God. God answers the prayer of the repentant (James 5:16).

Is God answering your prayers? Whom do you know who is committing sin? Can you pray for them? God still says we are to marry only believers.

Thursday · HAGGAI 1:1-15

DIGGING DEEPER • After coming out of bondage, the Jews were excited to start rebuilding the temple for worship, but soon their focus began to turn from God's house to their own houses. God wasn't pleased with their selfishness, lack of commitment, and ungrateful spirits, so the Lord cut off the blessing. Their clothing failed to keep them warm, they were running low on water and food, their crops and cattle were weak, and it was as if their money was going into pockets with holes. God used Haggai the prophet to tell them to turn their priorities back to the Lord. Most people listened, and God began to bless and change the hearts of the people.

Are you more concerned with your own things and plans, or with God's? Remember, God is still using His Word and people to help us focus on things above.

Friday · HAGGAI 2:1-9

DIGGING DEEPER · It's been about seven weeks since the Jews began their work on the temple, and Haggai has another message from God. The first time he spoke just to the leaders; this time he spoke to everyone. This message was to tell everyone not to be discouraged, but to rejoice that God was in their presence and that God was keeping His promises from the days of Moses. The very fact that God was there with them was a sign of His approval and enablement. He reminded the people that God was the one who owned all the riches of the world, and that because of Him they had all the resources they needed to rebuild the temple. Therefore, they should have no fear: God's peace was near.
Is it comforting to know that God keeps His promises? Do you trust God to supply all your needs?

Saturday · HAGGAI 2:10-23

DIGGING DEEPER · We now have the third message from God to the people through the prophet Haggai. God reminded His people it was their lack of obedience in the past that had caused them to have so many difficulties in their lives. Now, because of their obedience, God assured them that He would bless them. The fourth message of Haggai was to Zerubbabel. This message would be life-transforming. God had chosen Zerubbabel, and would destroy all of the Jews' enemies while Zerubbabel led them. Zerubbabel received great reward even in the future, because he would be in the lineage of Jesus (*Zorobabel* – Matthew 1:13).
Isn't it good to know that we serve a forgiving God? If we serve God with pure motives, He will reward us beyond our expectations.

QuietTime

Have you ever had a real passion to do something? A passion so strong that you'd risk anything to see it accomplished...even if it meant your death? This week you'll learn of such an individual and what he was willing to risk. When it comes to serving God, what price tag will you put on your service to God?

Prayer focus for this week

THE QUESTION · *What is the writer saying?*
THE ANSWER · *How Can I apply this to my life?*

Sunday · NEHEMIAH 1:1-11

DIGGING DEEPER • What is your greatest accomplishment in life? Nehemiah, a Jew born in captivity, was about to be used of God to lead God's people in Jerusalem to do great exploits for Him. Nehemiah was the cupbearer (food tester) for the Persian king Artaxerxes. When he heard that the walls of Jerusalem (1,000 miles away) were torn down, he immediately fell to his knees, weeping. As a Jew, his heart was in Jerusalem. He immediately prayed and asked God what to do. His prayer had four parts: adoration (vv. 5-6a), confession (vv. 6-7), thanksgiving (vv. 8-10), and supplication (v. 11). That's a great pattern for us to use as well. **How do you respond when you hear of God's work and God's people in distress? How can you use Nehemiah's prayer outline in your daily quiet time?**

Monday · NEHEMIAH 2:1-8

Q

A

DIGGING DEEPER · Do you ever wonder if God is at work in the world... even in the hearts of unbelievers? This story will convince you that the king's heart is in the hand of the Lord (Proverbs 21:1). After a four-month prayer vigil, Nehemiah's face showed that something was wrong. When the king sensed it and inquired about it, Nehemiah told him of his broken heart over the run-down conditions of Jerusalem. Then God, through the king, granted Nehemiah all of his requests and more: letters, time, soldiers, timber, and the governorship of Jerusalem itself. What more could you ask for?

What is it that you are asking God for today? Is your request for the glory of God? Will you recognize the hand of God, even if He answers your prayer in a way you have never thought of?

Tuesday · NEHEMIAH 2:9-20

Q

A

DIGGING DEEPER · Has God called you into leadership? Nehemiah's example of leadership here is a model to be followed by God's people everywhere. God had put the desire to rebuild the walls into his heart. He surveyed the ruins with a few choice men. He presented his credentials as a man of God and presented the obvious problems. They responded, "Let us arise and build." There will always be opposition to the work of God (vv. 10, 19) but godly leadership can overcome these obstacles.

Is God impressing you to lead others to do a great work for Him (v. 18)? Is it obvious to others that God's hand is on you? How will you handle opposition to the work of God?

Wednesday · NEHEMIAH 3:1-16

DIGGING DEEPER • Has God given you the spiritual gift of administration? Nehemiah organized forty-two groups of workers. He kept families or natural groupings of people together. Each group had its own leader and its own stake in the process. Often they worked on the wall near their own homes or close to their workplaces. Although each group had its own work to do, each work was connected to the work next to it. Everyone worked as a team.

How are you doing in the work that God has assigned you to do? How are you cooperating with other workers in your own group, or in the "group next door"?

Thursday · NEHEMIAH 3:17-32

DIGGING DEEPER • Here is another way to look at the ten gates mentioned in chapter 3. The ten gates could represent the Christian life: (1) Sheep Gate (v. 1)—salvation (John 10:9, 11); (2) Fish Gate (v. 3)—witness (Matthew 4:19); (3) Old Gate (v. 6)—walk (Jeremiah 6:16); (4) Valley Gate (v. 13)—trials (2 Corinthians 4:17); (5) Dung Gate (v. 14)—confession (2 Corinthians 7:1); (6) Fountain Gate (v. 15)—spirituality (John 7:38); (7) Water Gate (v. 26)—the Word (Nehemiah 8:1); (8) Horse Gate (v. 28)—warfare (Ephesians 6:11); (9) East Gate (v. 29)—rapture (1 Thessalonians 4:17); (10) Miphkad Gate (v. 31)—inspection (2 Corinthians 5:10). Each was instrumental in the growth and safety of the city; so, too, with our lives.

Are you a growing Christian? Is your life being protected and transformed day by day through God's Word?

Friday · NEHEMIAH 4:1-9

Q

A

DIGGING DEEPER • Have you ever been mocked or criticized for something you were doing for God? Nehemiah refused to allow outside antagonizers to stop the work of God. He went immediately to prayer. His prayer was answered in the willingness of the people. They had a mind to work (v. 6), and they never stopped. They had a heart to pray (v. 9); they never stopped praying. But they also had an eye to watch (v. 9); they never stopped watching their evil enemies. As a result, they were doing God's work God's way, and that's the direction to go!

What does it take to stop you from doing the work of God? What lesson can you learn from Nehemiah when facing opposition? Do you have a willingness to work, a habit of prayer, and a watchful eye for the enemy?

Saturday · NEHEMIAH 4:10-23

Q

A

DIGGING DEEPER • Do you ever get overwhelmed? Sometimes discouragement comes into the hearts of believers, as it did here. The hard labor and constant threats had taken their toll. Nehemiah did two things to revive the workers' spirits. First, he told them that they were doing the Lord's work. Secondly, he armed them and told them to fight to protect their own families. This counsel got every worker back on the wall, building with one hand and ready to do battle with the other. Working and watching is a good formula.

What are you building for God? What are you battling to overcome? How have you handled your own discouragement? How does Nehemiah's counsel encourage you?

QuietTime

WEEK 25

What does it take to have true revival in a city? Nehemiah is busy with a whole lot more than building a physical wall around the city. God will use him in these final chapters to bring a whole city to a place of revival. God may be preparing you for a great work, too. Listen with your mind and heart as you finish this book.

Prayer focus for this week

THE QUESTION *What is the writer saying?*
THE ANSWER *How Can I apply this to my life?*

Sunday · NEHEMIAH 5:1-13

DIGGING DEEPER · Recent events have given us a visual glimpse into the conditions in countries like Israel and Afghanistan. The conditions in Jerusalem during Nehemiah's time were deplorable, and the greedy hearts of some of the Jews were making things worse. Leviticus 25:35-42 clearly outlines the rules concerning loaning money to fellow Jews. All of these rules were being broken, and Nehemiah was compelled to right the wrong in Jerusalem.

How did Nehemiah have the courage to confront evil among his own people? Are you sensitive to the troubles of those around you? Whom is God leading you to help today?

Monday · NEHEMIAH 5:14-6:9

Q

A

DIGGING DEEPER · Part of the secret to Nehemiah's spiritual power was his honesty before God and man. He was setting the record straight regarding his financial integrity and the public record of his generosity. Regardless of his sterling reputation, the enemy continually tried to get him to come down from his high vantage point to talk to them in the valley. Nehemiah saw right through their scheme and refused. Their attacks were outright lies that they hurled at him continually and publicly.

What steps have you taken to live a life above reproach in your finances? Have you been generous with others and honest with God? How do you respond to constant attacks from Satan when you set out to do something for God?

Tuesday · NEHEMIAH 6:10-19

Q

A

DIGGING DEEPER · Satan will use any means to stop us from doing God's will. A private meeting with a leader of the Jews was the next arena for trickery. Thankfully, Nehemiah was walking so close to God that he discerned Shemaiah's scheme to trick him into doing something wrong. Satan's tactic was fear. Notice how Nehemiah goes from reporting the facts to praying to God in a seamless fashion. The unbelievers were embarrassed when they realized that God was behind Nehemiah's work.

Are you sensitive to the Spirit of God, and are you aware when Satan is scheming to hurt you? Are you learning to pray without ceasing, as Nehemiah did?

Wednesday · NEHEMIAH 8:1-12

DIGGING DEEPER · The wall was completed just five days before four holy gatherings were to start on the first day of the seventh month (Leviticus 23:24). Nehemiah had prepared the people in chapter 7. Now the public reading of the Word of God would be the centerpiece of the great revival that would sweep Jerusalem. Ezra 7:10 tells how a teacher prepared to teach God's Word. Nehemiah 8:8 tells the method we should use to teach. The reading brought tears of repentance, which turned to great joy (Hebrews 4:12).

Do you see the great power in the Word of God? Maybe God has called you to be a teacher of God's Word, one who expounds the truth and causes others to understand. Find someone with whom to share the truths of this passage today.

Thursday · NEHEMIAH 8:13-9:3

DIGGING DEEPER · As they continued to read on the second day, the Jews realized that they had not observed the Feast of Tabernacles. They began to set up booths for each family. This was done in remembrance of their deliverance from Egypt. Finally, they finished the last "solemn assembly" (a day of confession and prayer) on the twenty-fourth day of the seventh month. By now, there was such a spirit of revival among this group of over 40,000 people that they continued to read for a quarter of a day and then confessed sins for another quarter part of a day. This led to the longest recorded prayer in Scripture. It was a prayer of national repentance.

What will it take to bring us back to God? How can you apply these great lessons of Scripture reading and repentance to your life today? Can you see the transforming power of reading God's Word day by day?

Friday · NEHEMIAH 12:27-43

Q

A

DIGGING DEEPER • The ministry of the Word and the repentance it produced led to a great promise (covenant) in chapter 10. The leaders signed it and made three great promises in 10:30-39. Nehemiah 11:1—12:26 lists the arrangements necessary to restore order to Jerusalem. The stage was now set for the great dedication of the wall and the restoration of the temple procedures. What an impressive scene this was, with two great choirs marching around the wall in opposite directions until they met. Then they gave praise to God for all that had been accomplished.

Is God using you, as He used Nehemiah, to lead God's people in great exploits for Him? Perhaps you see yourself in one of the dozens of other functions performed in these chapters. Have you taken time to thank God for what He has done in your life today?

Saturday · NEHEMIAH 13:1-14

Q

A

DIGGING DEEPER • The job of a spiritual leader never ends. Chapter 13 reports a later visit that Nehemiah made to Jerusalem, sometime after his twelve-year reign as governor. The people had broken their promises made in chapter 10. Nehemiah sets out to correct those wrongs. He was willing to do what was right even when doing right was difficult. You will need to remember that when you seek to do what's right, there will be plenty of opposition; some of it will be from unsuspecting friendly sources!

Has your love for Christ deepened over the years? What commitments have you made to Christ that need to be renewed? Nehemiah's life encourages all of us that God's way is the best way.

QuietTime

WEEK 26

Here in the first few chapters of Acts, the apostles witnessed Christ's resurrection and then His ascension into Heaven! Ten days later, the Holy Spirit empowered them to take the Gospel to the whole world, and the church was born! This book is packed full of exciting true stories about what God did in and through people.

Prayer focus for this week

THE QUESTION *What is the writer saying?*
THE ANSWER *How Can I apply this to my life?*

Sunday · ACTS 1:1-11

Q

A

DIGGING DEEPER · First things first. For 40 days after His resurrection, Jesus instructed and encouraged His disciples concerning the power of the Holy Spirit, which they would need and receive. He told them that His power was for witnessing. He even told them where they should go with their message of hope. Then, He ascended into Heaven as they all watched. Two angels reminded them that He would return in the rapture, just as He had ascended.

Are you bold as you witness for Jesus Christ? The power of the Holy Spirit is available to every Christian who asks God for it! Soon Jesus will come again. Are you ready, and is everyone you know ready, for Jesus to return?

Monday · ACTS 1:12-26

Q

A

DIGGING DEEPER · It would be hard to imagine all that was going through the apostles' minds. Jesus had just ascended to Heaven, so they walked the half-mile back to Jerusalem and went into the upper room with all the believers they knew. They prayed and then chose Matthias to take the place of Judas. After that, they waited for the power of the Holy Spirit to come. Jesus had promised Holy Spirit power in verse 8, so now they had ten days to wait before they would be filled with the power they needed in order to be bold witnesses for Jesus.

Have you prayed for the powerful filling of the Holy Spirit so that you can be a mighty witness for Jesus? These men were on the verge of being changed forever by God's power. Why not make this prayer of submission a daily prayer of yours?

Tuesday · ACTS 2:1-13

Q

A

DIGGING DEEPER · Jesus promised that the Holy Spirit would come to indwell the disciples, and just as He promised, the Holy Spirit came upon them 50 days after Jesus ascended. The church of the Lord Jesus Christ was established that day, and the proof of this power was the gift of tongues. This foundational gift (Hebrews 2:3-4) allowed all people in Jerusalem to hear the Gospel in their own language. The Gospel would now go into all the world because of this miracle. This sign gift of speaking in tongues, or known languages, has accomplished its purpose and is no longer necessary, since the Holy Spirit now dwells within each believer. We simply need to ask for His filling to empower us.

Are you sharing the Gospel with everyone around you in your school, your team, your neighborhood, and your world? Share Christ today.

Wednesday · ACTS 2:14-21

Q

A

DIGGING DEEPER · Did you ever wonder why God put you in certain situations, why you were born where you were, and why you have your looks, your intelligence, your interests, your race, and your friends? Peter, now filled with the Holy Spirit, knew exactly what to do in this situation. He was going to tell all these people about Jesus! God was at work and He was going to use Peter-the mumbling, bumbling, stumbling Peter-to preach the one sermon that would start the church! Life doesn't get any better than this!

God knows what He is doing in your life also! Isn't it exciting to know that God is still at work in this world to bring people to Himself, and He is using you to get that work done? Jump into the situation God has put you in today and speak up for Christ.

Thursday · ACTS 2:22-36

Q

A

DIGGING DEEPER · Did you ever try to win an argument with your best friend? To win, you have to start with what he already knows and take him to what he doesn't yet know. Peter is taking his best friends (the Jews) from what they know to what they don't know (vv. 22-24). They knew Jesus as a man. Peter is saying that His miracles prove He is God. In verses 25-31, Peter is telling them that Jesus Christ was the Savior and was promised through David's line. In verses 32-36, the Jews knew that Jesus had been raised from the dead. Peter lets them know that this resurrection proved that Jesus was God.

Peter's arguments are the same arguments we use today to let people know why we believe in Jesus. Find someone today and tell him how Jesus proved that He was God, and how He died and rose again.

Friday · ACTS 2:37-47

Q

A

DIGGING DEEPER • Peter is a fisherman. Now he draws the net, just like Jesus said he would when He said, "Follow me and I will make you fishers of men." Repentance is what you do to be saved, and baptism always comes after salvation. Isn't it amazing that 3,000 people were saved and baptized at the end of Peter's sermon? The church was born with 3,000 members, who immediately did all the things that healthy churches always do (vv. 41-47). What about your church? Is it healthy? **Are you involved in the ministry of your church? Jesus loves the church, and the church gives us all a place to do the things that matter the most to Him. Have you been holding out in an area of service?**

Saturday · ACTS 3:1-11

Q

A

DIGGING DEEPER • God was at work using miracles to get the Gospel out to the entire world. Notice how Peter and John were going about their regular weekly routine when God gave them a person with a prepared heart. Peter had miracle-working power, so his "such as I have give I thee" allowed a lame man to be healed. If Peter could witness and see lives changed, so can we. Today we have the same powerful life-changing Gospel of Jesus Christ. We can tell people about Jesus in the power of the Holy Spirit, and watch spiritual cripples walk! **Whom is God going to put in your path today as you go about your daily routine? Ask God to make you sensitive to His Spirit as He puts prepared hearts in front of you.**

QuietTime

WEEK 27

Do you want to be bold and courageous? Peter and the other apostles did things that they never imagined they could do through the power of the Holy Spirit. Watch the miraculous story continue to unfold in this week's quiet time.

Prayer focus for this week

THE QUESTION *What is the writer saying?*
THE ANSWER *How Can I apply this to my life?*

Sunday · ACTS 3:12-26

Q

A

DIGGING DEEPER · Peter is using his opportunities to witness and serve the Lord. Now he preaches his second sermon to the Jews, who are questioning his healing of the lame man. Look at his powerful, Holy Spirit-inspired words as he lays out the case against these men. They killed the Prince of Life and God raised Him up. Yet God was still offering them salvation, and even the kingdom, through repentance. Look at the beautiful offer of love in verse 26: "unto you first." Not only did God offer salvation to the Jews, but He offers it to everyone who believes (Romans 1:16).

Have you repented of your sins and been converted? What are you doing today to get this Gospel out to your world?

Monday · ACTS 4:1-12

Q

A

DIGGING DEEPER · Peter's second sermon had produced 5,000 converts, but now his message brings persecution. Any time God is at work, we know that our enemy, Satan, will be at work as well. He does his best to stop God's work and destroy God's people. Peter had previously denied Jesus in the house of Annas and Caiaphas (John 18). Now, filled with the Holy Spirit, he boldly proclaims Jesus as Messiah and the only name "whereby we must be saved." Living for Jesus is a supernatural business. God alone, through His Spirit, can give us the power to stand for Him.
Why not ask God to fill you with His Holy Spirit so that you will have boldness as Peter did? He will give you power to stand in any situation, or before any audience, or before any person you may see today.

Tuesday · ACTS 4:13-22

Q

A

DIGGING DEEPER · People who have been with Jesus can't stop talking about Him! It was obvious that the miracle of healing was real, because the man who had been healed was right there in the middle of the crowd of those who believed on Jesus. Also, these religious leaders picked up on the fact that Peter and John had been with Jesus and were the real deal. So, having no argument against them, they threatened Peter and John by commanding that they not speak in the name of Jesus. Peter and John boldly stated that they could not stop talking about what they had both seen and heard.
What about you? Have you been in trouble for speaking too much about Jesus? Why not try it this week? Just talk about Jesus everywhere you go. Use His name and watch the reaction of everyone around you.

Wednesday · Acts 4:23-37

DIGGING DEEPER • There was a constant need to be filled with the Holy Spirit. The task ahead of the early church was impossible for them to do on their own; they had to depend on the Lord to do it. So, they prayed for boldness and God gave it to them. This early church was filled with great power and a great amount of God's grace was on them all. Isn't this the way that our churches should still be today? Because the needs were so great, these people sold everything to care for the needs of the new believers. Perhaps our churches should learn a lesson from this as well.

What are you willing to give up for God? What are you attempting for God that can only be carried out if God empowers you to do it by His Spirit? God is looking for students who are fully yielded to Him. Will you be one?

Thursday · Acts 5:1-11

DIGGING DEEPER • God was showing off His church to the world. Ananias and Sapphira now become a stark example that the church is holy and should not be treated lightly. They lied to God, the Holy Spirit (v. 3). They agreed together to sin against the Spirit of the Lord. God's judgment was death for the couple. 1 Corinthians 11:30 shows that God sometimes takes His sinning children to Heaven when they don't behave themselves on earth. To Christians, it is written in Hebrews 10:31, "It is a fearful thing to fall into the hands of the living God."

Is there an area in your life in which you are disobeying one of God's clear commands? 1 John 1:9 gives us the path to forgiveness and restoration. Why not take advantage of God's "spot remover" when it comes to sin?

Friday · ACTS 5:12-23

Q

A

DIGGING DEEPER · God was working mighty miracles to validate the Gospel message. The death of Ananias and Sapphira and the healing of *everyone* who was brought to the apostles were causing so much trouble for the Jewish leaders that they decided to throw the apostles into prison. The Angel of the Lord performed another miracle by releasing the apostles in the middle of the night, and instructed them to go and speak "all the words of this life" in the temple. God has a message that He wants carried to the entire world, and He commands us to take it.

How is your Scripture memory this week? How about your Christian service? These disciplines give us opportunities to tell others about our wonderful Savior, Jesus Christ! Don't let anything stop you this week.

Saturday · ACTS 5:24-32

Q

A

DIGGING DEEPER · When the apostles were finally brought from the temple to the Sanhedrin, the story was the same. The apostles were going to obey God rather than men, and they could not stop talking about Jesus. The unbelieving Jews couldn't understand that the blood of Jesus was on their hands, but Peter made it clear to them that they were the ones who had killed Jesus and hung Him on a tree.

Just as those Jewish leaders were guilty of killing Jesus, so are we. It is our sin that put Him on that cross, and He willingly paid the price for our redemption. Why not thank Him right now for saving you from your sin through His sacrifice on the cross?

QuietTime

WEEK 28

One preacher said, "If you want power with God, then read the book of Acts." This week in your quiet time you will find story after story of weak men who became bold as lions because of the power of God's Spirit. Read these pages and pray that God will use and empower you as He did those ordinary men.

Prayer focus for this week

THE QUESTION *What is the writer saying?*
THE ANSWER *How Can I apply this to my life?*

Sunday · ACTS 5:33-42

Q

A

DIGGING DEEPER · The world wants to silence the Christian and even put him to death. God used Gamaliel, a religious Jew, to save the apostles' lives. They were threatened and beaten, and forbidden to speak in the name of Jesus, but when they were let go they rejoiced and started talking immediately about Jesus-publicly (in the temple) and privately (in every house). They were simply being what God asked them to be... witnesses. When God says GO, man cannot say STOP.
What does it take to stop you from talking about Jesus? Are you talking about Jesus publicly, privately, and at every opportunity?

Monday · ACTS 6:1-15

Q

A

DIGGING DEEPER • This chapter tells about the first seven deacons chosen to serve in the church. The deacons in our church today should have the same qualities as these godly men. Notice that they were men who had a reputation of honesty, and who were full of the Holy Spirit, and of wisdom (v. 3). By serving the needs of the widows, deacons allowed the apostles to pray, study, and preach the Word without distraction. Stephen, one of the first deacons, was so filled with the Spirit of God, he was singled out for persecution. Yet at the time of his death, he looked like an angel, even while being falsely accused.

God may call you, young man, to be a deacon (servant) in the church one day, or maybe He will call you, young woman, to be a deacon's wife (1 Timothy 3:11). Are you ready to be all that God wants you to be?

Tuesday · ACTS 7:1-16

Q

A

DIGGING DEEPER • Stephen, the deacon, preaches the longest sermon in the book of Acts. He proves his faith and his knowledge of the Scriptures as he traces Israel's history starting with Abraham. His message tells about the disobedience of the Jewish people all throughout their history, yet the goodness of God and His guidance of His chosen people are also told in story after story. Just as God was merciful and longsuffering toward Israel, so He is toward us today as well.

How is God leading in your life today? Do you see Him at work in the circumstances of your life? Are you following Him in obedience?

Wednesday · ACTS 7:17-29

Q

A

DIGGING DEEPER • Stephen's sermon continues, and he tells about the amazing life of Moses. God was working in the circumstances of Moses' life to develop him into a man whom He would use to deliver His people from slavery in Egypt. Moses was sinful and fearful, yet God chose to use him for a purpose much bigger than himself. If He can train and use someone like Moses, do you not think He can do the same for us? Is anything… or anyone, too hard for God?
What is God preparing you for today? God never makes a mistake when He grows us into the men and women He wants us to be. Ask God to use you to do great things for His glory.

Thursday · ACTS 7:30-43

Q

A

DIGGING DEEPER • Stephen continues his sermon and uses the story of Moses to show the rebellion of the children of Israel. God wasn't finished working in Moses' life, even though Moses had been in the desert for 40 years. God was able to convince Moses that he was sufficient to lead and guide the Israelites out of captivity in Egypt. But the Israelite travelers were hard to lead, and they constantly complained and wandered from God. They even worshiped idols! This was a convicting sermon for Stephen's listeners, and has applications for us today.
How are you doing following God-given authorities in your life? How are things between you and your parents, your teachers at school, and your leaders at church? Are you obedient and teachable, or are you like the children of Israel?

Friday · ACTS 7:44-60

Q

A

DIGGING DEEPER • It has been said that "the blood of the martyrs is the seed of the church." Stephen finished his one and only sermon by applying the truth to those who were listening. They so hated the truth that they stoned him to death! But Jesus stood up to greet him in Heaven. Also in this passage, Saul (Paul) comes into the picture. God was using the death of this saint, Stephen, to spread the Gospel and send His church to the ends of the earth!

Would you be willing to speak the truth, even if it would take you to your death? Most of us will never have the opportunity to die for Christ, but we have the privilege to live for Him every day of our lives! Are you willing to live, or die, for Him?

Saturday · ACTS 8:1-13

Q

A

DIGGING DEEPER • Because of Stephen's stoning, a full-scale persecution of Christians breaks out in Jerusalem. Now the Gospel spreads north into Samaria (Acts 1:8), and will eventually go to the uttermost part of the earth. The spotlight that had been on Peter will now focus on Saul, soon to be named *Paul*. The first missionaries are mentioned in verse 4, and the first hypocrite (someone who pretends to be something he is not) is mentioned starting in verse 9. What a contrast! Today we get to choose which ones we will follow: Peter and Paul, or the hypocrites.

Whose side are you on? If this were only a football game, it wouldn't matter, but Heaven, Hell, and eternity are not a game. Everything is important, and everything we do counts forever. Have you decided to go all out for Jesus Christ?

QuietTime

WEEK 29

Is your world filled with people who seem impossible to reach? This week you will read about the Gospel affecting a devil worshiper, a powerful treasurer of a nation, a possible religious murderer, and a military officer. The Gospel can touch the hardest heart, so it can touch the hearts of your friends.

Prayer focus for this week

THE QUESTION — *What is the writer saying?*
THE ANSWER — *How Can I apply this to my life?*

Sunday · ACTS 8:14-25

DIGGING DEEPER · This is a key passage to help us understand miracles and sign gifts in the New Testament. Philip had been performing miracles and many people were believing on Jesus and being baptized. Then Peter and John came down from Jerusalem, and the Holy Spirit was given to these new believers. Miracles of healing and tongues were performed by the apostles to validate the Gospel message. These sign gifts were necessary at the time to validate the message; the Bible was not yet complete, and people needed signs to know that the message was true and intended for both the Jews and the Gentiles. We should all want the power of God, but not for the false reasons that motivated Simon.

God's power is never given to a person to show off, but only for God's glory. What do you want God's power for?

Monday · ACTS 8:26-40

Q

A

DIGGING DEEPER • Did you ever feel that God was asking you to leave your group of friends and reach out to someone who was alone? God led Philip out of a great revival meeting in Samaria to witness to one prepared heart out in the desert. The eunuch was a man of great authority who had been looking for God in Jerusalem and couldn't find Him. Philip found Jesus right in the pages of Isaiah (53:7-8) and led the man to Christ. He was ready to be baptized because he believed that Jesus Christ was the Son of God. Believe and be baptized; how simple it is.

Are you a soul winner like Philip? Are you listening to the Holy Spirit as He leads you to witness to people who are out of your comfort zone? Why not pray right now and ask God to give you a person with a prepared heart to whom you can witness today?

Tuesday · ACTS 9:1-9

Q

A

DIGGING DEEPER • Of all the people you know, who do you think is the most unlikely to get saved? If you were living back during the time of these writings, you would think it was Saul of Tarsus! Since nothing is too hard for God, He did just that. He saved Saul of Tarsus. Saul hated Christians, and thought he was serving God by persecuting them, and even killing them! He knew that the bright light that blinded him had to be the Lord; he just didn't know His name. Can you imagine how surprised he was when the Lord said "I am Jesus"? He was saved when he asked "Lord, what wilt thou have me to do?"

The Gospel is the power of God unto salvation. God is saving people and changing their lives all over the world. Has He saved and changed you? Have you found out what He wants you to do with your life?

Wednesday · ACTS 9:10-22

DIGGING DEEPER • God uses different people in our lives to lead us into His will. Ananias was first afraid for his life, but he obeyed God and went to Saul to pray for him to receive his sight. Not only did he obey God, but he called Saul "brother." God's will for Saul was beyond imagination: he was to carry the Gospel to Gentiles, kings, and the children of Israel. Paul was filled with the Spirit, baptized, and immediately began preaching that Jesus Christ is the Son of God. Sometimes when God saves a person, He puts him to work immediately bragging on Jesus! **What are you doing with your salvation? Are you telling everyone you know how wonderful Jesus is? Why not write out the testimony of your salvation and share it with someone today?**

Thursday · ACTS 9:23-31

DIGGING DEEPER • Saul learned to walk alone with God. He spent three years in Arabia and came back as a spiritual powerhouse. The only way this could have happened is by reading the Scriptures and spending time in prayer with God. We need to make regular time with God in prayer and Bible study (Quiet Time) a priority as well, so we can be changed like Saul. Barnabas stuck up for Saul when no one believed that he was the real deal. The churches protected Saul and had rest as they started multiplying. See Galatians 1:17-24 to read about this time in the life of Saul from another viewpoint. **How is your quiet time? Do you see God helping you grow privately today for a more public role tomorrow? Why not be a Barnabas to a new Christian today?**

Friday · ACTS 9:32-43

Q
A

DIGGING DEEPER · The spotlight now turns back on Peter. The Gospel is being shared freely and the apostles are moving freely between the churches in Jerusalem, Judea, Galilee, and Samaria. The apostles had great miracle-working power that was used to spread the Gospel. Every time they performed a miracle, people were brought to the Lord (vv. 35, 42). Now Peter moves into the house of Simon the tanner, a man who cured animal skins. This was a place a Jew would not normally go, but it was God's launching pad for the church to go to the uttermost part of the earth (Acts 1:8). The Gospel is adequate for everyone, everywhere, anytime. **Are you fully surrendered to God to go anywhere and do anything He wants you to do? The world has yet to see what God can do with a man or a woman who is fully yielded to Him.**

Saturday · ACTS 10:1-8

Q
A

DIGGING DEEPER · The amazing story of the first Gentile being converted to Christ now unfolds in these verses before us. Cornelius is a Roman officer in charge of 100 men. His heart is seeking God, but he doesn't know where to find Him. God is now at work in the life of Cornelius to get a soul winner to him so he can hear the Gospel and become a Christian. He would seem like an unlikely person to become a convert, but God had other plans! The Gospel message is adequate to save both the Jew and the Gentile (all those of other nationalities), and Peter had the privilege of carrying this message of hope. **Do you ever wrongfully judge a person? Are you ready to share the Gospel with the person you know who is least likely to be saved? Could God possibly be calling you to take the Gospel to another land or culture?**

QuietTime

Acts is the Power Book of the Bible. Story after story shows God's mighty hand at work in the world. From Cornelius' miraculous salvation to Peter's release from prison, we see the mighty hand of God working to get the Gospel to the ends of the earth. Be prepared for more exciting news as other lives are being changed.

Prayer focus for this week

THE QUESTION *What is the writer saying?*
THE ANSWER *How Can I apply this to my life?*

Sunday · ACTS 10:9-22

DIGGING DEEPER • God was changing Peter's heart about salvation. Peter thought that only Jews could be saved, but God now shows him that the Gentiles can be saved, too. Tradition is one of the biggest hurdles we face (for example, "we've always done it this way"). The vision of the sheet full of unclean animals and the instruction from God to "kill and eat" breaks down all the Jewish traditions that Peter has practiced. Now the men appearing at the door to take him to Cornelius complete the story.

Are you sensitive to God's working in people's hearts to hear the Gospel? Are you ready to obey today when the Holy Spirit says to your heart, "Witness to that one"? Are you actively involved in getting the Gospel to people who need Christ?

Monday · ACTS 10:23-33

Q

A

DIGGING DEEPER • If we only knew the work that God was doing in the hearts of people, we would be more willing witnesses. God led Cornelius to call for Peter. God led Peter to go to Cornelius. Peter had to act on what the Spirit had led him to do. God was breaking down Peter's prejudice (v. 28) and was bringing a large group of family and friends into the kingdom (vv. 24, 33). The stage was now set for the power of the Gospel to take over!

Are you expecting a divine appointment today? Pray right now and ask God to make you willing and available to witness to the prepared heart He sends your way today.

Tuesday · ACTS 10:34-48

Q

A

DIGGING DEEPER • Peter's message to Cornelius was the same message that *we* would share in a one-on-one witnessing experience. People must believe that Jesus is God (v. 36). He is also completely human (v. 38). He lived a perfect life, He was crucified, He was buried, and He rose again on the third day and was seen of many witnesses (vv. 39-40). Peter tells them that he saw Christ alive (v. 41). The requirement for salvation is shared in verse 43: "whosoever believeth." Immediately, this whole group of Gentiles believed on Jesus, and a scene like Pentecost (Acts 2:4) occurred again. This was God's way of proving to Peter that He was now saving Gentiles, just the same way He had saved Jews who believed. Just like Saul's conversion, baptism was the first step of obedience.

To whom could you witness who is different than you? Will you?

Wednesday · ACTS 11:1-15

DIGGING DEEPER • Sometimes Christians who do not witness do not understand what God has done. Peter had to explain to the new Jewish believers in Jerusalem what had happened at Cornelius' house. The plan of God was unfolding, but it had to be explained step-by-step to everyone. Peter took time to think it through and prepared his message (v. 4) so that he convincingly shared the story of God's dealings in this case, and shared his own argument that God gave the Gentiles the same sign that the Jews received on the day of Pentecost (v. 15).
Are you ready to share your story with others? When you share your story, be sure to always brag on Jesus! Tell how the Lord worked in your life and give all the glory to Him.

Thursday · ACTS 11:16-30

DIGGING DEEPER • Peter finishes his testimony about the salvation of Cornelius in verses 16-18. Truly, this salvation was an act of God alone. The rest of today's verses center on the church at Antioch. This special church became the sending church for the Apostle Paul (still named Saul here). Barnabas was a key leader and continued to be a friend to Saul as he set out to find him and minister with him. We should all desire to be like Barnabas, who was still witnessing and believing in Saul as he had always done (9:27). The visit mentioned here is spoken of in more detail in Galatians 2:1-10.
Have you surrendered yourself to God to go anywhere and do anything He wants you to do? God is at work in all kinds of people, in all kinds of ways, to get the Gospel out. Are you using all of your gifts for the glory of God?

Friday · ACTS 12:1-11

Q

A

DIGGING DEEPER •   James was the first of the apostles to be martyred. The evil Herod Agrippa thought it would make him even more popular with the Jews if he also killed Peter. Now Peter is in prison at this time, but God is not ready for Peter to come to Heaven yet. Peter himself doesn't even know what God is doing. In fact, he thinks his miraculous jail release is a dream. He finally realizes that he wasn't dreaming, and that God really was at work in this situation all along. When it comes to one's salvation or deliverance, it's always good to know that you know.

Do you ever wonder why God allows one Christian to die and another to live? God has a specific purpose and plan for every life. We will know all of these answers when we get to Heaven. Do you realize that God is actually at work in your life, and His working is not just a dream, but a reality?

Saturday · ACTS 12:12-25

Q

A

DIGGING DEEPER •   Now we're in John Mark's house (v. 12), where Peter arrived and broke up the prayer meeting. Answers to prayer sometimes catch even believers off guard. John Mark would eventually go on the first missionary journey with Paul and Barnabas (v. 25). Herod, unable to accept the fact that God had supernaturally allowed Peter to escape, had the soldiers executed. Then he went to Caesarea, where he was proclaimed a god and promptly eaten by worms because of his pride. God will not be mocked, nor share His glory. He will have His way in this world. Anyone who sets out to put himself in the place of God should beware!

Do you ever wonder how your prayers would be answered if they were prayed in faith? Have you seen the mighty hand of God at work in the world around you? Why not ask God in faith to meet your needs today?

QuietTime

WEEK 31

In every area of our lives there is someone in charge to whom we have to answer. This week we see how Paul and Barnabas answer the call to go preach the Gospel. They preach the truth when they are persecuted and stoned, and they get counsel from those in authority over them when they have questions.

Prayer focus for this week

THE QUESTION · *What is the writer saying?*
THE ANSWER · *How Can I apply this to my life?*

Sunday · ACTS 13:1-13

Q

A

DIGGING DEEPER · All of us at one time or another have been in a situation where someone was choosing teams. One *captain* chooses, and then the other, and so on until everyone is on a team. In today's passage we have a very distinct choice from God. The Holy Spirit Himself said, "Now separate to me Barnabas and Saul for the work to which I have called them." Paul and Barnabas already belonged to Christ and were hard at work serving the Lord in Antioch (v. 2). He had additional plans for them to go out and preach the Gospel and tell people about Christ. Notice that these men were not waiting around for some glamorous position; they were servants doing all they could for the Lord. **List two things you can be doing for the Lord right now to serve Him. List two ministries in which you would like to serve the Lord in the future.**

Monday · ACTS 13:14-25

Q

A

DIGGING DEEPER • Sometimes we can't wait to hear news of something that affects us, like the outcome of an election, or whether we've made the team, or passed Driver's Ed. We wait impatiently for any news that will tell us what we are dying to know. Paul loved to tell people about Christ and to remind the Jews of the exciting news that Jesus was the Christ they had been looking for all these years. Paul's desire was to show that the coming of Christ Jesus was not an accident in God's program, but rather the fulfillment of His righteous plan. That plan was evident even in the choosing of David to be king, because it was through David's descendants that Jesus was born.

What three things about Jesus Christ encourage or excite you the most? Which of these will you tell someone else about this week?

Tuesday · ACTS 13:26-41

Q

A

DIGGING DEEPER • God doesn't make mistakes; if He did, then He wouldn't be God. Paul makes that point very clear in today's passage. Three times (verses 27, 29, and 33) Paul emphasizes that the things that happened to Jesus Christ were not a mistake. Rather, they all happened according to the prophetic plan of God. This was an important point to Paul, and should be to us. God always intended that Jesus should die as He did. It was part of God fulfilling His promise. The importance of Christ's death, burial, and resurrection is seen in verses 38 and 39 where Paul reminds his readers that without Christ's sacrifice there would be no justification and no salvation from sin.

Have you ever questioned an area of your life in which you thought God had made a mistake? What helped you get through it?

Wednesday · ACTS 13:42-52

Q

A

DIGGING DEEPER • When people lose their sight, it makes everyday life almost impossible. Blind people do not see or understand the world around them like they did when they had sight. Spiritual blindness not only blinds a person's heart and mind, but it seeks to impose this blindness on others as well; so it was with the Jews in Antioch of Pisidia. They not only rejected the Gospel themselves; they also did not want anyone else to accept it. It was for this reason that Paul and Barnabas were called out by the Holy Spirit to take the Gospel to the Gentiles. Blind people would accept the gift of sight if it was offered to them, but the Jews did not want to see and understand, and therefore forfeited a great privilege.

One reason God saves us is so we can tell others of His salvation. Who have you told? List three people you should tell. Will you do it this week?

Thursday · ACTS 14:1-13

Q

A

DIGGING DEEPER • Most of us have never had to run for our lives, but every once in a while we say or do something that will get us in big trouble, and we find ourselves looking for a quick exit in order to survive. Paul and Barnabas were spreading the Gospel in Iconium, and unbelieving Jews didn't like it, so they tried to turn the crowd against them with lies. Paul and Barnabas were no dummies; they left the city, only to step into more chaos. The people of Lystra and Derbe thought that Paul and Barnabas were the gods come to earth, because they had healed a crippled man. With much persuasion and common sense Paul told the people about the true God, and that he and Barnabas were just men here to serve Him.

What can we say and do that will make it clear to people who the true God is? Who will you speak to today?

Friday · ACTS 14:14-28

Q

A

DIGGING DEEPER • Have you ever had one of those days when no one seemed to understand you? Things started out bad for Paul and Barnabas, and then got worse! They walked right back into the mess when they got to Lystra, because the Jews from Antioch and Iconium had come there and persuaded the people that Paul was bad news. So the people stoned Paul with rocks and left him for dead. But while the disciples who were in Lystra gathered around Paul, he got up and went into the city (v. 20), and the next day he and Barnabas left for Derbe. It is only through God's protection that Paul survived the stoning and lived to preach another day.
List three ways God protects you or provides for you so that you can tell others about Christ.

Saturday · ACTS 15:1-12

Q

A

DIGGING DEEPER • Have you ever wondered about some of the traditions you have at your church, and why they do certain things the way they do? Paul and Barnabas found themselves in the middle of a controversy that took them to the high counsel in Jerusalem. Circumcision in the Old Testament was God's indication that His people, the Jews, were set apart unto Him. The Gentiles were not circumcised but were still trusting in Christ as their Savior; so the question had to be answered: Is circumcision necessary for salvation? Peter gives a good defense against requiring Gentiles to observe Jewish rituals. Peter's point was that if the Holy Spirit accepted Gentiles apart from the Law and circumcision, why should we as men try to require it?
What does Scripture say is required of us to be saved?

QuietTime

WEEK 32

Remember when you did a project at school or helped someone build something? It takes time. There are many things to consider, and if you give up midway, nothing is accomplished, you flunk, or the structure goes undone. This week we will see the importance of not giving up when things are tough.

Prayer focus for this week

THE QUESTION · THE ANSWER

What is the writer saying?
How Can I apply this to my life?

Sunday · ACTS 15:13-29

Q
A

DIGGING DEEPER · From the Middle East to the local playground, we all have to decide that we will need to give up certain freedoms if we are going to live and work together with people who are different than we are. In today's passage, the cultures of the Jews and Gentiles were in conflict because Christian Jews still practiced some of their cultural traditions. The Gentile Christians didn't understand why they needed to follow such practices; circumcision being the main point of contention. James and the council from Jerusalem sent word by Paul and others that the Gentile Christians did not need to follow all the cultural habits of the Jews, but there were a few things (v. 29) that would promote unity among all believers.

List two things at home which you and your family have agreed to do to "be at peace" with each other. List two such things from school or work, also.

Monday · ACTS 15:30-41

Q

A

DIGGING DEEPER · Remember the last time you had a disagreement with a person and needed someone to mediate, or you agreed to disagree and remain friends? Paul and Barnabas had just such a disagreement over taking Mark (who later wrote the Gospel of Mark) with them on this missionary journey, because he had quit and gone home the last time they were together. Paul chose Silas, but Barnabas took Mark, and the two pairs went to minister to different people. Because Barnabas worked with Mark and gave him another chance to prove himself, Mark became useful to God and Paul in the ministry (2 Timothy 4:11 and Philemon 23-24). One failure is not total failure. God can change us and use us, no matter what.
Who deserves another chance in your life? How often has the Lord forgiven you and given you another chance?

Tuesday · ACTS 16:1-13

Q

A

DIGGING DEEPER · Every one of us has uttered that famous phrase, "I don't want to." Many mothers respond with, "Well I do a lot of things I don't want to do." The reality we have to live with is that, in order to accomplish what we want in life, there are many things we have to do that we don't necessarily want to. Timothy was a godly young man whom Paul had discipled and wanted to take along with him (v. 3) but first, he needed to be circumcised so he wouldn't offend the Jews in that area. Timothy was willing to do something that he did not necessarily want to do so that the Gospel would go forth. Also in this same passage, Paul was directed by the Holy Spirit to go where he had not intended, yet he obeyed anyway.
List two things you've seen your parents or other believers do for Christ that were inconvenient. List two tough things that you should be doing.

Wednesday · ACTS 16:14-24

DIGGING DEEPER · It would make quite a headline if we were to read one day that a local drug lord was using the money he got from selling drugs to feed the hungry and build houses for the poor. The problem with this picture is that profit from something illegal is always wrong, no matter what *good* someone tries to do with it. Paul met a woman who was demon possessed and was a fortune teller. She spoke the truth about Paul, saying that he was God's servant proclaiming salvation, but she was still demon possessed. Paul was not about to allow a demon, through the slave girl, to promote his ministry. That would look like Paul was in cooperation with demons, which was just not true.

Are there things in which you are involved that may look like they are good causes, but in reality do not serve the best interests of Christ?

Thursday · ACTS 16:25-40

DIGGING DEEPER · Sometimes we suffer because we do what is right. Daniel did, when he was thrown into the lion's den for praying to God. Christ suffered and died because the Jews did not like His message that He was God, the Son. Paul and Silas were beaten and put in prison because Paul cast out the demon in the slave girl, causing her owners to lose money. Instead of being upset that their rights were being violated, Paul and Silas sang hymns and prayed (v. 25). God sent an earthquake that loosed all the prisoners. The result was that Paul was able to witness to the jailer and lead him to Christ. When people see we handle tough situations and trust the Lord instead of getting mad, they may often ask us why.

Do people see your trust in the Lord? Are you different than others when it comes to worry and trust? Has anyone ever asked about your faith?

Friday · ACTS 17:1-9

Q

A

DIGGING DEEPER · What we say and do always affects more than just us. Paul and Silas went into the synagogue to teach who Christ was, and many Jews and Gentiles believed. But the Jews who did not believe were jealous because people believed Paul rather than them. They later started a riot, which endangered the welfare of one of the new believers, named Jason. We are not told all that happened to him other than that he was charged a fine and let go. Paul, out of consideration for his friend, decided to leave the city at night. The Christians did not give up, though. They shared their faith and the Church grew, in spite of opposition.
Do something different today. Go to 1 Thessalonians and read all of chapter 3 so you know the whole story of God's faithfulness.

Saturday · ACTS 17:10-21

Q

A

DIGGING DEEPER · When we watch our favorite sports teams play, we realize that to be their best, they cannot give up or quit. After Paul, Silas, and Timothy were thrown out of town, they left Thessalonica and went to Berea to preach the Gospel. They were not about to give up spreading the good news of Christ. It wasn't long before the Jews from Thessalonica followed them and stirred up trouble in Berea. So Paul went to Athens and began to reason with them (v. 17) concerning Christ and His resurrection. The Greeks were deeply interested in knowing all they could about everything, so they sought out Paul and listened closely to what he had to say about Christ (vv. 20-21), giving Paul opportunity to spread the good news.
List three opportunities God has provided for you to tell others about Christ even when it has been hard.

QuietTime

WEEK 33

In a courtroom, if you do not tell the truth you can be put in jail. When we know the truth about something, it keeps us from making mistakes. The chapters in this week's study are a reminder of the importance of knowing the truth about Christ and living our lives based on that truth.

Prayer focus for this week

THE QUESTION — *What is the writer saying?*
THE ANSWER — *How Can I apply this to my life?*

Sunday · ACTS 17:22-34

Q

A

DIGGING DEEPER · Many of us believe that in real life we will never need to know those miserable math formulas we learn in school. Others love mathematics and can calculate anything in an instant. We don't start out in first grade doing calculus; the simple leads to the complex. We start from what we know in order to learn what we don't know. Paul did the same thing with the people in Athens. They had a statue with the inscription "TO THE UNKNOWN GOD." They knew that God was out there, but they didn't know Him. Paul showed them truths they didn't know by using ones they already knew, and taught them that God is the Creator, Provider, in control of all things, and the One who provided salvation from sin.

List two or three ways you can use known principles to tell people what they don't know about Christ.

Monday · ACTS 18:1-17

Q

A

DIGGING DEEPER • Every one of us likes to know when we are doing something right. We either get paid for it, someone compliments us on a job well done, or we get a bonus, etc. Paul met opposition to the Gospel message he was preaching, but he never got discouraged. He determined that if some would not hear him and believe, he would go to those who would. An added encouragement to Paul was that the Lord spoke to Paul in a vision telling him to not be afraid, and to continue to speak the truth, because Christ was with him. Christ told him that no one would attack him or hurt him, and encouraged Paul with the fact that there were many believers in Corinth (vv. 9-10).

List two ways the Lord has encouraged you this past week in your service for Him. Whom can you encourage in the same way?

Tuesday · ACTS 18:18-28

Q

A

DIGGING DEEPER • There are times when we hear only part of a story or see the first part of a program, and part two is next week. A similar thing happened to a man named Apollos in today's passage. He had heard John the Baptist teach the need for repentance, and Apollos understood the Scriptures and taught them accurately (v. 25) and boldly in the synagogue. What he had not yet understood was the importance of salvation through Christ alone, because he had not yet heard the rest of the story. Aquila and Priscilla took Apollos aside and carefully instructed him concerning Christ. Apollos was used by God to refute the Jews, showing them from Scripture that Jesus is the Christ (v. 28).

Today's lesson is a good reminder of how we are to patiently help new believers understand more about Christ. Whom do you need to help?

Wednesday · ACTS 19:1-10

Q

A

DIGGING DEEPER • It is a wonderful thing to know that God provides what we need. Often we are reminded of this when He provides money we need, or our parents get a better job, or someone we pray for is cured of cancer. For the 12 men in today's passage, God provided them with truth, and he used Paul, His servant, to deliver that truth. John the Baptist preached repentance from sins. Christ taught the same, but also taught that faith in Him was required for salvation. Another provision God made for these men is the Holy Spirit, who indwelt them at the moment of their conversion. Notice that the purpose for speaking in tongues was to confirm the authority of the man of God and the work of God in his ministry.

God expects us to know the truth so that we can tell others. What four things would you tell someone who was inquiring about Christ?

Thursday · ACTS 19:11-22

Q

A

DIGGING DEEPER • Have you ever walked past a dog and thought it was a *nice doggie*, and then found out later that the smile on its face was from scheming about how to eat your leg? In Ephesus, there were certain men who thought it would make them popular if they could cast out demons in the name of Christ, as Paul had done (v. 13). The demon they encountered, seeing they had no authority, gave all seven men at once a good thrashing. The result of this event served only to settle a godly fear (respect) over Ephesus and magnify the Lord Jesus. There are many today who do not believe the truth, yet try to deceive people into believing that they have authority from God. It is important that we know the difference.

The way we can know who is really teaching the truth is to compare what is being taught with the truth of Scripture. How much do you know?

Friday · ACTS 19:23-41

Q

A

DIGGING DEEPER · Remember the last time you were around a kid who pitched a fit because he didn't get his way? It may be annoying, but in some cases it's funny. But the reality is that the child is selfish by nature and thinks that if he doesn't get what he wants, he has the right to kick, scream, and get angry. Paul had preached the Gospel for over three years, and many people in the area had turned from serving the goddess Diana to serving Christ. Those who sold idols of Diana were losing money, so they pitched a fit, brought two of Paul's friends into the theatre and accused them of turning people away from Diana. God used the logical argument of the city clerk (v. 35) to calm the crowd and protect His servants. **Take some time right now, and throughout the day, to pray and ask the Lord to show you where you want your way instead of His way.**

Saturday · ACTS 20:1-12

Q

A

DIGGING DEEPER · The believers in verse 7 met on the first day of the week– Sunday. This was done because it was the day of Christ's resurrection. Most Christian churches meet on Sunday for this reason, not because it is the Sabbath Day of the Old Testament. One commentator notes that Scripture does not require Christians to observe the Saturday Sabbath: 1) The Sabbath was the sign of the Mosaic Covenant, and Christians are under the New Covenant; 2) There is no New Testament command to keep the Sabbath; 3) The first command to keep the Sabbath was not until the time of Moses (Exodus 20:8); 4) The Jerusalem Council (chapter 15) did not order Gentile believers to keep the Sabbath; and 5) Paul never cautioned Christians about breaking the Sabbath. **Why do you go to church? List three reasons why church is so important.**

QuietTime

WEEK 34

When someone is hiring workers, he looks for people who are dedicated, dependable, and will follow directions. The Lord expects the same from us and Paul is a great example. This week we will see the importance of being loyal to Christ and following His leading in our lives.

Prayer focus for this week

THE **QUESTION** *What is the writer saying?*
THE **ANSWER** *How Can I apply this to my life?*

Sunday · ACTS 20:13-24

DIGGING DEEPER · When the Lord has work for us to do, we must keep at it. If we don't get the rest we need and stay healthy, we are of little use to God and the work He has for us. Paul had a goal of going to Jerusalem (v. 22) and Jesus confirmed that goal by His statement to Paul in Acts 23:11. We can take a lesson from Paul, who did not settle for just teaching and discipling a few people. He had a desire to reach many, and it was that desire, that vision and compassion for people, that motivated him to go and tell them about Christ. Christ encouraged His servant by telling Paul in a vision that he would be His witness in Rome, too.
List two things that you could be doing to serve the Lord in your church. List two things you can do at home that also would be serving the Lord.

Monday · ACTS 20:25-38

Q

A

DIGGING DEEPER • We are all familiar with tests and quizzes. Mid-terms and finals keep us up nights while we cram our heads full of information in order to get a good grade. Paul summarized his ministry as he examined his work with the people in that area. He told the church elders that he had no regrets; he had served as God had intended. He presented a summary of all he had done, and then he exhorted the elders to "examine" themselves, test themselves, and take inventory of how they were watching over and protecting their congregations (vv. 28-29). Paul likened the false teachers of the day to wolves, emphasizing the importance of being on the alert. **God expects us to be on the alert so we can help our Christian friends live for the Lord. We should pray for them and encourage them.**

Tuesday · ACTS 21:1-14

Q

A

DIGGING DEEPER • We have all seen someone who never gives up, whether it is someone running in the Olympics or someone recovering from an injury. Paul understood what it meant to keep going and not give up. He was determined to go to Jerusalem and preach the Gospel as Christ wanted him to (23:11). The Spirit revealed to the believers at Tyre that Paul would go to Jerusalem and face persecution. They were concerned for their friend, but after much conversation they were convinced, as Paul was, that this was God's will. In verse 14 they finally said, "The will of the Lord be done." The Lord surrounded Paul with believers that supported him and encouraged him in his service for Christ. **Ask your pastor or a parent to give you the e-mail address of at least two missionaries to whom you can write and give encouragement, then do it.**

Wednesday · ACTS 21:15-26

Q

A

DIGGING DEEPER • We often find it hard to understand different cultures. People from other countries have traditions that sometimes are quite different from ours. Paul has gone "up" to Jerusalem (Jerusalem is elevated on a plateau) to give a good report about the many Gentiles who have trusted Christ and are being discipled (v. 19). There were some who were spreading false reports that Paul was teaching Jewish believers to forsake their heritage. This accusation is seen to be false simply by observing Acts 16:1-3 and 18:18. The Jerusalem elders proposed a way by which Paul could demonstrate his loyalty to the traditions (vv. 23-24). Paul did not want to offend anyone, and followed their advice.

List two situations you can think of in which you or a friend had to follow someone else's rules to keep the peace.

Thursday · ACTS 21:27-40

Q

A

DIGGING DEEPER • Confusion among liars is common; they seldom get their story straight, and it causes chaos. This is the scene in today's passage where all of Jerusalem is in an uproar (v. 30). When the frenzied crowd was trying to beat him to death, Paul was rescued by a Roman tribune. This was the highest-ranking official stationed at Jerusalem. The garrison was comprised of 1,000 men. The Egyptian (v. 38) was a false prophet who, several years earlier, had promised to drive out the Romans. Before he could do so, however, his forces were attacked and routed by Roman troops led by Governor Felix. Lysias assumed Paul was that Egyptian, but Paul identified himself and was allowed to speak to the people.

Even though many people are yelling loudly that they are right, that doesn't make it so. Those who are right often speak softly and with control.

Friday · ACTS 22:1-16

DIGGING DEEPER • As Paul addresses the false charges brought by the Asian Jews, he speaks to the people in their own language. The first accusation is shown to be false, as Paul was a Jew but had been brought up in Jerusalem. The second accusation is shown to be ridiculous, as Paul had been a student of the most celebrated rabbi of the day, Gamaliel. Paul would have received extensive instruction in the Old Testament Law and Jewish traditions. Verse 16 has caused concern to some, but is better understood by reading it so that "calling on the name of the Lord," precedes "arise and be baptized." Salvation comes from calling on the name of the Lord (Romans 10:9-13), not from being baptized.

Paul takes opportunity to give his testimony as evidence of Christ's work in him. To whom can you tell your testimony this week?

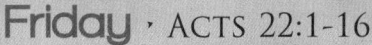

Saturday · ACTS 22:17-30

DIGGING DEEPER • Most people love to hear how the Lord has been faithful in people's lives and blessed them and watched over them. Paul gives such an account of his salvation and God's direction. Paul claims to have received direct revelation (in his trance) from Jesus Christ. The *trance* experience was unique to the apostles. Only Peter in Acts 10:10 and 11:5 and John in Revelation 1:10 had similar revelations. Paul's insistence that the Lord had sent him to minister to the Gentiles is too much for the crowd. Because of racial prejudice, the Jews could not accept the teaching that Gentiles could be saved without first becoming followers of Jewish traditions.

Is there someone to whom you won't talk about Christ because of race or religion? Ask God's forgiveness and go be a witness for Christ.

QuietTime

WEEK 35

Even as teenagers, there are times when we can feel our lives are out of control. We can't find a job, school is tough, our parents are having problems or are already divorced, and we don't know what to do. This week we will be reminded of how God uses all things to bring about His will.

Prayer focus for this week

THE QUESTION   *What is the writer saying?*
THE ANSWER   *How Can I apply this to my life?*

Sunday · ACTS 23:1-10

Q
A

DIGGING DEEPER · Ananias was one of Israel's cruelest and most corrupt High Priests. His actions so alienated him from the Jewish people that, at the revolt against Rome in A.D. 66, the people murdered him. The illegal act (see Deuteronomy 25:1-2) of striking Paul would be in keeping with Ananias' character. This was a vicious blow, not simply a slap on the face. Paul had come to Jerusalem to continue to preach the Gospel and give witness of Christ. He cleverly caused the Pharisees and Sadducees to argue over whether Paul was right regarding the resurrection of the dead. The argument led to Paul being taken into custody by Roman soldiers. That night Christ told Paul he would go to Rome to be His witness.
Christ tells us clearly that we are to tell others about Him. What keeps you from believing that God can use you to witness for Him?

Monday · ACTS 23:11-22

Q

A

DIGGING DEEPER • We often wonder how many times the Lord has worked in our lives to protect us, or has put a thought in our minds to do something in service for Him. In today's passage there were Jews that hated Paul so much that they made a vow they would not eat until they killed him. Paul's nephew was in the right place at the right time, led by the Lord to be there. When he told his uncle (Paul) of the plot against his life, Paul had him taken to the commander, who listened to the whole story, took the threat seriously, and gathered troops to protect Paul once again. God had a plan for Paul and there wasn't anything or anyone who could change that plan.

Ask your parents or grandparents to remember at least two times when the Lord protected them. Write one down for yourself.

Tuesday · ACTS 23:23-35

Q

A

DIGGING DEEPER • Lysias, with knowledge of the planned assassination, realizes his need to get Paul out of Jerusalem and to his supervisor, Felix. Felix was residing at Caesarea. The fact that Lysias sends half of his garrison shows just how serious the plot against Paul may have been. Every step in this process brought Paul in contact with more people of authority to whom he could witness. He was able to witness to Felix and to plead his case before the Jews once again in chapter 24. Paul was truly innocent, and the letter (vv. 26-30) written by Lysias to Felix spelled that out. Thus, Felix had no reason to suspect Paul of breaking Roman law, but only the laws of the Jews, which Rome did not enforce.

Each of us needs to pray for courage as we have opportunity to stand up for what is right even among adults in authority.

Wednesday · ACTS 24:1-16

Q

A

DIGGING DEEPER · It is very frustrating when someone lies about us and then other people believe it. Paul was accused of violations against Roman law and Jewish law. The first was the most serious before the court, as the Romans would not tolerate rebellion or those who promoted it. Had the Jewish leaders been able to substantiate this charge, Paul would have faced severe punishment—possibly even execution. The second charge against Paul was that he was a ringleader of the Nazarenes and a desecrater of the temple. Tertullus used the term "Nazarene" to describe believers, hoping that Felix would look upon Jesus' followers, like Paul, with disfavor.

Write down the three or four points from Paul's defense (vv. 10-16) that will help us in response to someone who lies about us.

Thursday · ACTS 24:17-27

Q

A

DIGGING DEEPER · Politicians often tell only some of the facts, to make themselves look better than their opponents. Paul tells the truth to Felix, and Felix understands. The real point for this trial was the dispute between the Sadducees and Pharisees (v. 21), who had different views on the issue of the resurrection. Obviously, Paul's belief in the resurrection was not a crime under either Jewish or Roman law. The court is adjourned pending more information from Lysias, but there is no evidence that Felix ever summoned him. Felix and his wife talked to Paul, who reminded Felix that he needed to be righteous and have self-control. Felix obviously felt conviction from this statement, and told Paul to go away.

Paul was innocent and the Lord protected him. Felix had sin in his life and felt guilty. What sins do you need to confess today?

Friday · ACTS 25:1-12

Q

A

DIGGING DEEPER • When we look back at our lives we can see many times when the Lord was with us and helped us. The same is true for our parents and grandparents, who have lived longer. In Paul's life, we see that Festus was also under God's control, and that his decisions brought about God's will for Paul and for those in Rome whom God wanted to reach with the Gospel. Festus was a good ruler and judge, and when he asked Paul if he was willing to go back to Jerusalem to be judged, he was trying to do a favor for the Jews. Paul refused, knowing that they would only try to kill him again (vv. 2-3). Paul was a Roman citizen, and it was his right to appeal to Caesar, which he did in verse 11.

We can know what God is doing in our lives when we look to His Word for help. List two things that keep you from reading your Bible.

Saturday · ACTS 25:13-27

Q

A

DIGGING DEEPER • Even though it is Saturday, today we have a history lesson in the relationship between the Jews and the Roman Empire. Festus spoke of the events leading up to the present occasion, including Paul's refusal to go up to Jerusalem to be judged, choosing rather to appeal to Caesar. "Augustus" (v. 21) refers to the Roman emperor, Nero. Festus' dilemma was deciding what explanation to give for sending Paul. To send a prisoner to the emperor without proper charges was both foolish and potentially dangerous. Festus is hoping that King Agrippa, with vast knowledge in Jewish affairs, can help to formulate the charges.

Notice all that these men go through to judge Paul, and all the opportunities Paul gets to witness for Christ. Will you take advantage of opportunities to witness?

QuietTime

People don't pick up a book and start reading it in the middle. If someone is in the middle of a good video, we wait until later to watch it from the start so we can catch the point of the film. We see from the accounts of Paul's ministry this week that from beginning to end, Christ had a purpose for Paul, just as He does for us.

Prayer focus for this week

THE QUESTION — *What is the writer saying?*
THE ANSWER — *How Can I apply this to my life?*

Sunday · ACTS 26:1-18

Q

A

DIGGING DEEPER · When we are thinking of getting a new video game or renting a DVD, we ask our friends to see if it's worth getting. Word-of-mouth is the best seller. Paul uses that same approach. He is not afraid or intimidated by Agrippa because he loves him and wants him to become a believer. Paul appeals to Agrippa's knowledge and expertise of Jewish customs. It must be remembered that Paul is not on trial here, but is being given an unbelievable opportunity to give his testimony. In fact, Paul's purpose here is to see Agrippa and others converted (vv. 28-29). Paul gives account of his pre-conversion, his upbringing, and the fact that he lived as a Pharisee. He speaks of the hope of the promise of the resurrection.

Pray right now and every day this week for the Lord to give you courage to talk to a specific person for whom you've been burdened.

Monday · ACTS 26:19-32

Q

A

DIGGING DEEPER • It is hard sometimes to give a gentle answer to someone who is accusing us or calling us names. Often, we want to retaliate and make the accuser look bad. Paul is gracious with Festus, and merely continues to state the truth. Festus interrupts the testimony of Paul and declares that all of his learning has driven him mad. Paul, with gentle tact, shows himself not to be mad. He informs Festus that what he has said about Christ and His resurrection is common knowledge in Palestine, and that he believes that King Agrippa fully understands the validity of what he has been saying. Agrippa is really saying, "Do you think you can convince me to become a Christian in such a short time?"

Pray and ask the Lord to give you control over your tongue and emotions so you can show compassion for people in a gentle way.

Tuesday · ACTS 27:1-13

Q

A

DIGGING DEEPER • Today's passage is another history lesson, with just a few facts to help us understand the time progression of Paul's journey to Rome. The return of the pronoun "we" marks the return of Luke as a traveling companion. A Roman citizen like Paul who appealed to the emperor would be treated better than most prisoners. Stopping at Sidon, Paul is permitted to visit his friends. The friends are part of a church that was probably established during the persecution that followed the death of Stephen (Acts 7:54-60).

Take time to talk to an older person from your church who has stories about God's faithfulness in his life. TAKE NOTES. Can you relate to any of the stories?

Wednesday · ACTS 27:14-29

Q

A

DIGGING DEEPER · Verse 14 describes a violent storm. The tempestuous wind was called Euroclydon, meaning "east wind and north wind." It was a strong and dangerous wind, and was greatly feared by those who sailed. This wind was part of the divine purpose to fulfill Jesus' words to Paul that he should testify of Him as Lord before Caesar. The lightening of the ship in verse 18 is the throwing overboard of all unnecessary gear and cargo to enable it to ride higher on the waves. Paul encouraged the crew that not only would he appear before the emperor, but that they all would survive for his sake.

How we handle tough times is an indication of our character and trust in God. Trust grows through testing.

Thursday · ACTS 27:30-44

Q

A

DIGGING DEEPER · The sailors intended to flee without helping the soldiers and prisoners sail the boat, so Julius cut the life boats free, preventing the sailors from getting away. Paul encouraged all the men to eat. With the inherent difficulty of food preparation during the storm, little or nothing had been eaten in the previous two weeks. Paul told the men that they all would survive (v. 34). Luke adds that there were 276 people on board—this was not a small ship. At that time, Roman soldiers who lost their prisoners were executed, so the soldiers on the ship planned to kill the prisoners rather than let them escape. Julius took command of a bad situation and told the soldiers not to kill their prisoners, but to get to shore.

List three indications that God is in control of all these circumstances in this passage.

Friday · ACTS 28:1-16

Q

A

DIGGING DEEPER • There will be many times in our lives when the Lord changes our plans and we have to wait for Him, but He always expects us to keep serving, even when plans change. Paul did just that for three months (v. 11) on the island of Malta. A snake bit Paul while he gathered sticks for a fire. It is obvious that the snake was poisonous, by the response of the natives watching to see when Paul would die. Certainly, Paul's survival was due to God's miraculous intervention. God used this incident once again to validate Paul as His messenger. During the next weeks, God worked many miracles at the hands of Paul. This was certainly done so that the people of Malta could come to believe the Gospel.

Don't ever quit working for the Lord. Always be ready to serve Him even when you are uncomfortable. Christ needs faithful servants.

Saturday · ACTS 28:17-31

Q

A

DIGGING DEEPER • Paul, under house arrest, can't leave to go to the people, so God has the people come to him! The interesting thing here is that the Jewish leadership willingly comes to hear Paul. Evidently the accusations against Paul have not yet spread as far as Rome. Paul's defense of the Gospel goes from morning until evening. Paul proclaims the Gospel by explaining, testifying, and persuading. In so doing, he appeals to the intellect, emotions, and will. Some are persuaded, but others do not believe (v. 24). The Book of Acts is a critical link between the Gospels and the Epistles, which explains how transitions of the Bible occur.

Thank the Lord for preserving His Word so we can better understand His work in the world. Why not seek to hand out a Gospel tract, a portion of God's Word, today?

QuietTime

The nation of Israel has left Egypt and is preparing to journey on toward the Promised Land. Now that the people have received instructions concerning the law and the tabernacle, they are ready to journey on. How's your journey going? Are you learning to trust God along the way?

Prayer focus for this week

THE QUESTION   *What is the writer saying?*
THE ANSWER   *How Can I apply this to my life?*

Sunday · NUMBERS 1:1-4, 44-46

DIGGING DEEPER • When the Israelites left Egypt, they were only a few days' journey from the Promised Land. Because of their disobedience and disbelief, God led them into the wilderness. Twelve and a half months later, God instructed Moses and Aaron to number all the men who were able to go to war. The total number was 603,550 men. It is tragic that out of these men, only 2 lived to enter into the Promised Land. Their names were Joshua and Caleb. If each of us could only learn to trust God and depend completely on Him, then our journeys would be easier and our blessings multiplied. Sometimes we fail to do so because we get so distracted by the things and circumstances around us.

Is your walk easy or hard? What has caused you to doubt God? Is there anything that God can't handle?

Monday · NUMBERS 1:47-2:2

Q

A

DIGGING DEEPER • God chose the tribe of Levi for a special work. Instead of going to war, they would be responsible to take care of all things concerning the tabernacle. They would set it up and take it down when it was time to move. No one else except the Levites could help with these responsibilities. The interesting fact about the tabernacle is that it was mobile. The Israelites took it with them wherever they went. This was their place of worship. God should be the focal point of all that we do and all that we are. We should be able to worship and praise Him wherever we go. As we wage warfare against the devil and all his schemes, praise God for pastors, youth pastors, and lay leaders who take care of our spiritual needs. **Do you ever thank God for your pastors, Sunday school teachers, or Discipleship leaders? How have they impacted your life?**

Tuesday · NUMBERS 3:1-16

Q

A

DIGGING DEEPER • Verse 4 tells us that Aaron's two sons, Nadab and Abihu, died because they offered "strange fire" before the Lord (Read Leviticus 10:1-2). God wants true worshipers-people who worship Him from their hearts and with the right motives. These men offered inappropriate sacrifices to God, much as Cain did (Genesis 4:5). God has prescribed certain standards for man to follow concerning our relationship with Him, and He takes those instructions very seriously. Some people want to worship God in their own ways. This does not honor God; instead, it grieves Him. It cost these two men their lives. **Are you worshiping God from your heart? Do you ever stop to think about who God really is? How are you preparing to serve Him?**

Wednesday · Numbers 3:38-50

DIGGING DEEPER • When the tenth plague fell upon Egypt, all the firstborn males were slain; however, the firstborn of Israel were spared (Exodus 12), and from that time forward, God claimed all firstborn males as His own (Exodus 13:2). The Levites were to be set apart for a purpose. So God commanded Moses to substitute the 22,000 Levite males for the firstborn of all Israelites one month old and up (who numbered 22,273). Each of the remaining 273 Israelite firstborn was to be redeemed for five shekels of silver (approximately $3.15) at one month of age (Numbers 18:15-16). Presenting the firstborn to the Lord acknowledged the fact that God is the giver and sustainer of all life. He created us, and while we were yet sinners, He redeemed us through the precious blood of His Son, Jesus.

Have you given yourself to the Lord? Read Romans 12:1-2

Thursday · Numbers 6:1-8, 22-27

DIGGING DEEPER • A Nazarite is one who has voluntarily separated himself unto the Lord. There were three requirements for anyone who chose to do this: First, they were to abstain from all alcoholic beverages and from anything that came from the grapevine. Next, they were to not cut their hair during their separation. Finally, they were to separate themselves from anything dead. God did not require anyone to take this vow, but those who did so must do it seriously. In many ways, believers are like the Nazarites. There is an offer to all to have a closer walk with the Lord. You must want it! It is an act of dedication. Read Romans 12:1-2 again.

Would you be willing to give up something to show how serious your dedication to the Lord is? To whom are you really dedicated? Why do you do what you do?

Friday · Numbers 7:1-9, 84-89

Q

A

DIGGING DEEPER • Moses is holding a service of dedication for the tabernacle. This is where people would come to meet God and have their sins forgiven (atoned) by the offering of sacrifices. The princes of Israel are the leaders of each tribe. They were listed in Numbers 1:5-15. Today's chapter is about the gifts that these men brought to the Lord. If you read the whole chapter, you will notice that even the smallest of gifts were recorded (vv. 14-16). You see, it doesn't matter how much we give. Big or small, the Lord accepts all gifts. What really matters is the heartfelt attitude of the giver (Luke 21:1-4).
How often do you give to God? Do you give your best? How much does God really deserve from us?

Saturday · Numbers 8:5-18

Q

A

DIGGING DEEPER • The Levites were set apart by the Lord (v. 14) to help with the ministry. They were to be cleansed by a one-time sprinkling of water, and also by the daily cleansing of their garments (v. 7). This twofold cleansing pictures the need of every believer to be washed by the blood of Jesus Christ and to daily cleanse himself through the washing of water by the Word of God (Ephesians 5:26) that they might serve with garments of righteousness (Colossians 3:12). The Levites were redeemed by God and made fit for His use. So are all who trust in the finished work of Jesus Christ.
Have you been washed in the blood of the Lamb of God? Are you spending time in God's Word on a daily basis? How has God cleaned up your life?

QuietTime

WEEK 38

This week we will see how a journey of faith begins to turn into one of doubt and disobedience. Sometimes the length of the journey will cause us to lose focus. If we are not careful, we will begin to murmur and complain. Let's not forget how much God has done for us and how far He has brought us.

Prayer focus for this week

THE QUESTION · *What is the writer saying?*
THE ANSWER · *How Can I apply this to my life?*

Sunday · NUMBERS 8:19-26

Q

A

DIGGING DEEPER · God gave to Aaron, the high priest, helpers consecrated for service to the ministry (v. 19). They would offer sacrifices for the atonement of the sins of Israel, so that they might come before the presence of God without fear of death. The word *atonement*, or as someone put it, "at-one-ment" (bringing us into a personal relationship with God), means *a covering*. Animals sacrificed according to the law provided a temporary covering for the confessed sins of the people; God's judgment for sin would be transferred to an innocent animal. When God offered His innocent Son on the cross, a permanent covering for sin was made. The judgment for our sins was transferred to Jesus. All we have to do is accept what God has already done for us through Jesus.

Have you considered how great a sacrifice God made for you?

Monday · NUMBERS 9:1-5, 15-23

Q

A

DIGGING DEEPER • The purpose of celebrating the Passover was to remind Israel of what God had done for them back in Egypt (vv. 1-14). God continued His presence in their lives through the pillar of cloud by day and the pillar of fire by night (vv. 15-23). He guided and protected the Israelites during their wilderness journey. Believers today do not need God's presence in a cloud. He is already ever-present in us. The Holy Spirit resides within all believers. He guides us and teaches us all things concerning His Word (John 14:26). We are instructed by the Holy Spirit as we read and study God's Word.

Does the Holy Spirit live in you? Do you follow His guidance? Are you searching for answers in the Word of God?

Tuesday · NUMBERS 10:1-13, 33-36

Q

A

DIGGING DEEPER • The sounding of trumpets had an important role to play for God's people in the past, and will again in the future. Verses 2-10 contain six different uses of the sounding of trumpets: 1) To call all the leaders together, 2) To assemble everyone at the tabernacle, 3) To assemble all able men for war, 4) To instruct armies to march, 5) To announce a holy convocation, and 6) To announce the beginning of a new month. One day, at the Rapture, the sound of a trumpet will play an important role in the life of all believers as Jesus gathers all believers in the clouds to take them to Heaven (1 Thessalonians 4:16). That is going to be one exciting event!

What about you? Are you listening for that trumpet to sound? What if it sounded today? Are you ready?

Wednesday · NUMBERS 11:4-17

Q

A

DIGGING DEEPER • Up to this point we have seen a people obedient to God, but things are about to change. The Israelites started complaining, and God was displeased, even angered (vv. 1-3). Complaining and murmuring are like wildfire. Just a little spark and soon it's out of control. Even Moses began to complain to God (vv. 11-15). He was so beside himself that he asked God to kill him. From where did this complaining come? Verse 4 tells us that it was those of the "mixt multitude," who had followed the Israelites out of Egypt. They had a lust for the things of Egypt, and their complaining was beginning to spread.
What has God provided for you? Do you complain in spite of His provision? Are you careful not to let the murmuring of others cause you to sin?

Thursday · NUMBERS 11:18-25, 31-33

Q

A

DIGGING DEEPER • It was only a short journey of eleven days to the Promised Land, a land flowing with milk and honey. Israel would only have to endure eight more days, but because of their complaining, the journey came to a stop for an entire month. Their own unbelief caused them a longer journey. They demanded more to eat than just bread. God had miraculously provided their food, yet they were not happy. If they would have trusted God, just a few days away would be more food and more variety than they could ever have asked for. God always knows best, yet we crave more. That's the same as saying, "God, we don't want what you give us; we want something else or something more." Shame on us!
Make a list of the things you really want. Are they what God wants? Are you ignoring His blessings because you want more?

Friday · NUMBERS 12:1-15

Q

A

DIGGING DEEPER • Miriam and Aaron were disturbed that Moses' wife was not a Hebrew. They were also disturbed that "little brother" was exercising authority over them (vv. 1-2). After all, Aaron was 3 years older than Moses, and he was the high priest. Miriam was also Moses' elder, and a prophetess. God overheard Miriam and Aaron, and was displeased with their complaining (v. 2). Moses was God's man, appointed to oversee God's people. God will deal with those who come against a man of God (v. 10). We should give much respect and attentiveness to those whom God has chosen to lead us (Hebrews 13:17).

Do you ever envy those who have authority? Do you show respect for your pastor? What might God do to those who disrespect their spiritual leaders?

Saturday · NUMBERS 13:1-3, 16-25

Q

A

DIGGING DEEPER • Israel had finally arrived at the Promised Land. It was time for them to go in and possess it. However, the people thought that it would be a good idea to send spies into the land to search it out first (Deuteronomy 1:20-22). While this was not God's idea, He allowed them to do so (v. 1). Keep in mind that God already told them that the land was theirs to possess. All they had to do was go. Sending spies into the land was a sign of weakness, doubt, and fear on the part of the people. It would have been better to trust God. After 40 days, the spies returned with good news and bad news. Tomorrow we will find out about this news.

Do you completely trust God? Why is it better to believe God than to give in to our fears? How are faith and fear different?

QuietTime

WEEK 39

The nation of Israel has arrived at the Promised Land, and all is just as God had promised. However, there is one problem. There are reports of "giants" in the land, and fear has overtaken God's people. What will they do? What do you do when fear and doubt come? Do you trust God, or are you like the Israelites?

Prayer focus for this week

THE QUESTION — *What is the writer saying?*
THE ANSWER — *How Can I apply this to my life?*

Sunday · NUMBERS 13:26–14:5

DIGGING DEEPER · Twelve men went to spy out Canaan land. They saw that the land was plentiful and just as God had promised (v. 27). But ten of them brought back an evil report because all they could see were the giants (vv. 28-29, 31-33). Only two men, Joshua and Caleb, brought back a good report (v. 30). The people began complaining and rebelling against God (14:1-4). God had already promised the land to them. Victory was theirs! All they had to do was obey Caleb's advice: "Let us go up at once, and possess it; for we are well able to overcome it" (v. 30). Instead they believed and followed the majority. This display of doubt, fear, and disobedience cost them their blessing…and their lives. All but two, Joshua and Caleb, would die in the wilderness.
Are you missing God's blessings because of doubt, fear, or disobedience?

Monday · NUMBERS 14:6-19

Q

A

DIGGING DEEPER · The reaction of Moses, Aaron, Joshua, and Caleb was that of great sorrow (vv. 5-6). They pleaded with the people to trust and obey God. These four men knew that rebellion against God's specific calling was a grievous sin (1 Samuel 15:23). Rather than fearing God's judgment, Israel feared man. They rejected the pleading of their leaders; therefore, their fate was set. God would have destroyed them all on the spot had Moses not intervened on their behalf (vv. 12-19). We should praise God that He is a patient and longsuffering God. Many times He has had the right to destroy us, yet His great love for us compels Him to pour out mercy and grace that we don't deserve.
Have you ever rebelled against God by disobeying His Word? Why should God forgive you? Aren't you glad that He does?

Tuesday · NUMBERS 14:20-33

Q

A

DIGGING DEEPER · God is patient and He does forgive, but He always deals with sin. We serve a holy God who deserves honor, glory, and praise. He also deserves our obedience, and, regardless of whether or not we give it, He will be glorified (vv. 20-21). God had grown tired of Israel's disobedience, and now He dealt with it (vv. 22-23). Those who rebelled against God were forgiven, but they were still disciplined. As a result of their disobedience, they would never see the Promised Land. The inheritance had been taken away and given to their children (v. 31). All God really wants from you and me is faith. He wants us to trust Him completely. Why shouldn't we trust Him? He is God! (Read Hebrews 11:6.)
Do you have faith in God? How can you show God that you trust Him? Can you please God without faith?

Wednesday · NUMBERS 14:34-45

Q

A

DIGGING DEEPER • Earlier in this chapter (v. 2), the people of Israel said they would have rather died in Egypt or in the wilderness than to face their fears in the Promised Land. They were about to get their wish! Because of their disobedience they would spend 40 years in the wilderness and die without entering the Promised Land (vv. 34-35). When Israel was confronted with her sin, the people mourned greatly and confessed their sin (v. 40). However, they still followed their own hearts, and when they attempted to enter the land by their own power, they were defeated and many were killed (vv. 44-45). If we want success in this life, we must learn to trust and obey God's Word. If we try to do it our way, we will fail.
Whose counsel do you follow? The world's? Your own? Or God's? Are you studying His Word to find His will?

Thursday · NUMBERS 15:22-36

Q

A

DIGGING DEEPER • All those who disobeyed the Lord would be unable to receive the promise, but God did not abandon His plan to establish the descendants of Abraham, Isaac, and Jacob in the land He promised them. The Lord began to set up rules of worship and conduct so that the people could remain in a right relationship with Him. If they sinned, a sacrifice was to be offered to obtain forgiveness. There were different standards for different sins (vv. 24-31). If the people followed God's rules, their sins would be forgiven. However, there was no sacrifice for those who sinned willfully after receiving the truth (see also Hebrews 10:26). Even the most terrible sins can be forgiven if there is true repentance.
Can you see how dangerous it is to know the truth, yet reject it? What sin do you need to deal with? Why not deal with it today?

Friday · NUMBERS 17:1-11

Q

A

DIGGING DEEPER · In chapter 16, a rebellion arose against Moses and Aaron. A man named Korah convinced many that Moses and Aaron were taking authority that God had intended for all the people (v. 3). He also blamed Moses and Aaron for the people's failure to enter the Promised Land. God destroyed Korah and his followers, as well as 14,700 people who complained against Moses and Aaron. In today's passage, God proves to the people that Aaron can be trusted as the high priest of Israel. Aaron's rod was later placed in the Ark of the Covenant as a reminder to all the people (Hebrews 9:4). It is never a good idea to rebel against a man who has been called of God. Those who do so also rebel against God.

How well do you submit to those in authority? Do you murmur or rebel against them? Does it please God when you do?

Saturday · NUMBERS 20:1-12

Q

A

DIGGING DEEPER · Can you believe that the people are complaining again? Neither could Moses and Aaron. They fell on their faces before God (v. 6). Instead of judgment, God graciously provided what they needed. Moses however, learned a painful lesson in all this. God told Moses to speak to the rock (v. 8). Moses became so exasperated that, in a fit of anger, he struck the rock not once, but twice (vv. 10-11). God wanted to teach the people to trust Him instead of complaining. The people missed the lesson. Their need was met by God's graciousness, not by Moses' anger and force. This episode cost Moses his ticket to the Promised Land (v. 12). We must take care that in our frustration over the faults of others, we don't also fall into sin.

Are you a complainer? Does it make your situation better or worse?

QuietTime

WEEK 40

40 years have passed, and Israel is about to enter the Promised Land. A new generation of leaders and people are now ready to enter in. Israel has learned much during this long journey, and still has much to learn. In spite of distractions, disobedience, and doubt, God lovingly disciplines and blesses His people.

Prayer focus for this week

THE QUESTION *What is the writer saying?*
THE ANSWER *How Can I apply this to my life?*

Sunday · NUMBERS 20:23-21:9

DIGGING DEEPER · In yesterday's passage, and again today, we see that God is not partial to Moses and Aaron. They, too, lost their entry into the Promised Land because of rebellion (v. 24). At the age of 123 Aaron dies (33:39), and the priesthood is passed on to his son, Eleazar. Once again the people are tested, but this time they are victorious (21:1-3). When we trust God we will prevail. It is during those times of doubt and fear that we fail. The treacherous journey was beginning to discourage the people, and they murmured against God (vv. 4-5). So God sent fiery serpents into their midst, and many died (v. 6). The people recognized God's judgment and confessed their sins. When Moses intervened on their behalf, God provided a way for them to live (vv. 8-9).

How have you been tested? Are you moving forward with God?

Monday · NUMBERS 22:1-15

Q

A

DIGGING DEEPER · The King of the Moabites feared Israel. He feared that they would overtake him. Balak hired a prophet named Balaam to come and curse God's people, but every time Balaam tried to get God to curse them, He revealed wonderful future events concerning Israel. Balaam believed in the power of God. He prayed to God, and God spoke to him. When he spoke, he spoke God's Word. However, he served self instead of God. Through familiarity with God's Word, false teachers do the same today. The indwelling Holy Spirit is able to teach us from God's Word who is true and who is false. We must remain in God's Word so that we will know the truth from a lie. Today there are many who follow error and are being led astray. **How well do you know the Bible? Could you recognize false teachings? Have you heard any false teachings lately?**

Tuesday · NUMBERS 22:21-35

Q

A

DIGGING DEEPER · God was angry with Balaam because He had already told him not to go with these men (v. 12). Balaam already had an answer from God (v. 19). He knew God's will, but he wanted something different. Sometimes God will allow us to have what we want, even if it is not His desire for us. However, it is during times like these that we learn some very hard lessons. Balaam was too blind to see the angel in the way. It took a donkey seeing and speaking to get Balaam's attention (vv. 25-28). In spite of Balaam's perverseness, God still accomplished His own purposes. We should choose to be used by God as an example of obedience rather than an example of disobedience. **God used a talking donkey to get Balaam's attention. What does God have to do to get your attention? What kind of an example are you?**

Wednesday · NUMBERS 27:12-23

DIGGING DEEPER • The Lord showed Moses the Promised Land from Mount Abarim. He also told Moses that he would soon die (vv. 12-13). Moses asked God to set another man before the people to lead them (vv. 15-17). God revealed that Moses' successor would be Joshua (v. 18). Joshua was a God-fearing man full of the Spirit. He had been a faithful servant and leader among the people. The charge to Joshua by Moses is recorded in Deuteronomy 31:7-8. The laying on of hands symbolizes the transfer of authority from Moses to Joshua, and signifies honor to the new leader (v. 23). Every believer has the indwelling of the Holy Spirit of God. We have His help and His power at our fingertips.

Are you a leader? Could God ask you to lead? Are you preparing yourself for what God has called you to do?

Thursday · NUMBERS 32:1-15

DIGGING DEEPER • A new generation has come to the threshold of the Promised Land. They are now ready to enter in, but two tribes don't want to go across Jordan into the Promised Land. They would rather stay on this side of Jordan (vv. 1-5). The grass looks greener on this side for them. They seem to be saying, "We have heard of God's promise of a land flowing with milk and honey, but this is good enough for us." That's the same as saying that they don't want what God is offering. By staying, they can never receive God's full blessings, and their contentment to remain behind shows that their hearts are not wholly committed to God.

Have you settled for second best? Why would you want to stay here, when God is going over there and wants you to follow Him? Will you follow or stay?

Friday · NUMBERS 32:16-31

Q

A

DIGGING DEEPER · These two tribes were willing to be a part of God's program, but only on their (own) terms. Notice the use of the words "we will" and "we will not." Their minds were already made up. They were not asking for permission as much as they were looking for support in their decision. God allowed them to take up residence on this side of the Jordan, but there were some strong disadvantages to this decision. These two tribes were the first to fall into idolatry and the first to be taken into captivity (1 Chronicles 5:25-26). Many Christians today are possessed by their possessions. They are willing to sacrifice things of spiritual importance for this world's treasures and pleasures. These choices will make them weak.
Do your desires match God's will? Are you willing to give up your desires for God's will?

Saturday · NUMBERS 35:9-25

Q

A

DIGGING DEEPER · If someone was killed accidentally, the law provided a way of escape for the person who had killed him (Exodus 21:13; Numbers 35:11). Cities of refuge were appointed by God as a place for a killer to seek safety and protection until he had a chance to prove that he did not kill intentionally. If he was found guilty, he was put to death; if he was not guilty, then he was set free, and anyone who killed him was in danger of judgment. Jesus has become our place of refuge. Even though we deserve death for our sins, in Christ we find forgiveness and safety. "...who have fled for refuge to lay hold upon the hope set before us." He is our only "hope" and our only way of escape (Hebrews 6:18-19)!
Have you fled to Jesus for safety? Do you have any sin right now that you need to confess before Him?

QuietTime

WEEK 41

When someone has surgery, he is grateful that he can depend on the surgeon to do the job right. We want someone with experience who won't quit in the middle of the operation to go for a snack. This week we will learn the value of the integrity of God's Word and the integrity of the person who presents it.

Prayer focus for this week

THE QUESTION — *What is the writer saying?*
THE ANSWER — *How Can I apply this to my life?*

Sunday · GALATIANS 1:1-9

DIGGING DEEPER · A deserter weakens any army, hurts morale, and undermines the authority of the officers in charge. Desertion is so serious that, in some cases throughout history, deserters have been imprisoned, shot, or hung. In the opening verses to this book, Paul uses a strong description of the Galatians' actions, stating that he *marvels* at how quickly they have begun to remove themselves from the Gospel of Christ, turning to a false gospel taught by those who pervert the Word of God. Paul writes this letter with the intention of turning this process around (Galatians 5:1), reminding the churches of the influence that Scripture should have on them, and citing the authority of the Gospel he had already taught them (vv. 8-9).

Describe an occasion on which you have chosen to follow the truth of Scripture rather than the false teachings you hear every day.

Monday · GALATIANS 1:10-17

Q

A

DIGGING DEEPER • Reputation. Everybody has one. Even every nation on the planet has one. Our reputation is determined by our character, and it is seen and judged by everyone. Paul depends on his reputation as he answers his critics, who claimed that he was teaching one thing to the Jews and something different to the Gentiles. Paul did not receive the Gospel message from men (vv. 11-12) or from the apostles (vv. 16-17). The Gospel he taught came as a direct revelation from Jesus Christ. Paul had a close relationship with the believers in Galatia, and because they knew him, he could depend on his reputation to remind them that his authority came from the Lord, not from man.

Name a problem we create when we speak on our own authority rather than teaching from the truth of Scripture.

Tuesday · GALATIANS 1:18-24

Q

A

DIGGING DEEPER • When someone spends money on something of value, he wants to know he is getting the genuine article–the *real deal*. Everything from diamonds to vases to paintings, and even currency, is tested to prove that it is real. In today's passage, Paul defends his teaching and presents evidence that he ministers to people because of the authority given him by Christ, not by the words of other apostles. Paul's message was genuine; it came from Christ. And there were other people who rejoiced that Paul no longer persecuted Christians, but preached the very faith that he once sought to destroy (vv. 22-24). Paul's change of heart and his subsequent teaching were, in fact, the *real deal*.

What two things from today's passage can help us in our goal to properly relay truth in Christ's authority and not our own?

Wednesday · GALATIANS 2:1-6

Q

A

DIGGING DEEPER • Has anyone ever asked what was most important to you? Anyone who learns a new skill has to learn what the *main thing* is. We have all heard someone say, "Keep your eye on the ball!", "Concentrate!", "Take your time!", or, "Check your work to make sure you don't forget anything." To sum up all this wonderful advice, we could say, "The main thing is to keep the main thing the main thing." For Paul, the main thing was to make sure he taught people the truth about the Gospel of Christ. Paul willingly went and talked to the apostles at Jerusalem so there would be no misunderstanding about what he had been teaching. The apostles agreed with Paul's teaching and commended him for his faithfulness.
Do people know you are talking about the real deal? Do you have a life and love for God that backs up what you tell people?

Thursday · GALATIANS 2:7-14

Q

A

DIGGING DEEPER • There are ways we can tell who is on the same team in a soccer game. Which players are wearing the same color is a good clue. Another hint is when the ball is kicked into the goal and the players from that team create a body pile in the middle of the field, with their teammate on the bottom. Paul had the same purpose to preach the Gospel of Jesus Christ as did Peter, James, and John. The only difference was to whom they preached. Paul had been sent by God to the Gentiles, while Peter, James, and John were sent to the Jews. Each of them had the same purpose, power, and call from God. He just sent them to different people.
List two reasons that it is important for believers to present the Gospel to different people, instead of all of us going to the same group.

Friday · GALATIANS 2:15-21

Q

A

DIGGING DEEPER • In today's passage, Paul reminds the Galatians that justification and righteousness do not come from keeping the Old Testament Law, which was given to the Jews. Rather, they come only through belief in Jesus Christ, which was the very truth Paul taught. When someone was found guilty in court during Paul's day, he could be declared righteous by the judge only after he had worked off the debt of his offense. Our debt as sinners is impossible to *work off,* because it requires that we make a perfect sacrifice, which we cannot do. Paul admits in verse 20 that he has been crucified with Christ, and because Christ now lives in him, the life he lives he lives by faith in the Son of God.

Read verse 20 twice to yourself and then three times out loud, and remember Who saved you.

Saturday · GALATIANS 3:1-9

Q

A

DIGGING DEEPER • In a court of law, each side presents evidence in order to persuade the jury to its own way of thinking. The outcome depends on which side presents the best evidence in the best way, and convinces the jury. With this thought in mind, Paul asks the Galatians if they are truly so foolish as to believe that they could earn their salvation by works of the law, and then remain righteous by doing those same good works found in the law. Paul is asking them what evidence they have that would support such a conclusion. Paul reminds the believers that Abraham's righteousness was the result of his faith in God, not his own works, and that it is because of Abraham's faith that all the nations are blessed (v. 8).

Do you do good works because you have faith, or in order to have faith?

QuietTime

WEEK 42

No one likes the idea of being put in prison and losing the freedoms we enjoy. This week we will learn that the value of the Law in the Old Testament was to teach us of the freedom we have in Christ. Those who continue to live by Jewish Law forfeit the freedom they have in Christ, and choose bondage to the Law.

Prayer focus for this week

THE QUESTION · *What is the writer saying?*
THE ANSWER · *How Can I apply this to my life?*

Sunday · GALATIANS 3:10-16

DIGGING DEEPER · When a criminal is convicted, punishment follows. The sentence may be death or prison time, but there are always consequences. The *curse of the law* in today's passage signifies being handed over to the judgment and wrath of God. This is a serious thing, made worse by being linked here with the word *under* (v. 10). Rather than merely facing the possibility of a future punishment, *under* emphasizes that the follower of the Law is already subject to the wrath of God upon sin. The good news, however, is that Christ has redeemed us from the curse of the Law and, therefore, we are free from God's wrath. Christ paid our debt by dying on the cross and thereby buying our freedom.

List two of your friends who need to hear this good news. Think of the best way to tell them, and then pray for courage to do it.

Monday · GALATIANS 3:17-22

Q

A

DIGGING DEEPER · Promises, promises, promises! We hear them from everyone, but not many are kept. The word *promise* in Scripture means a *notification of agreement* or *to announce an intention*. Paul focuses in on God's promise to Abraham way back in the Old Testament, when God said, *In thee shall all nations of the earth be blessed* (Genesis 12:3). This promise was apart from the Law, which was given to Moses 430 years after God's agreement with Abraham. The promise God referred to in Genesis would be fulfilled in the future death and resurrection of Christ, who provided salvation for all. God always keeps His promises!

Name a promise to you that God has kept. What is a promise you have made to God? Have you kept it? Is there something you need to do to make it right, so that you keep a promise you've made either to God or others?

Tuesday · GALATIANS 3:23-29

Q

A

DIGGING DEEPER · It is not uncommon to have a tutor who helps us with a certain subject in school or gives us just a little better understanding of a topic. Paul refers to the Law as a schoolmaster or tutor that teaches us about Christ and our need for the justification He provides. The Old Testament taught the people of that day about God's righteous requirement, which they could not meet. But it is similar to taking Driver's Education today. You can take the class, read the book, and watch videos of what happens when people don't wear their seat belts, but eventually you will have to drive. The Old Testament Law doesn't save us; it just points us to Christ and our need for salvation through Him, but we still have to accept it.

Have you ever read an instruction manual but refused to follow it? How does this relate to knowing God's righteousness but never trusting Christ?

Wednesday · GALATIANS 4:1-7

DIGGING DEEPER • When it comes to privileges and authority, there are days when it seems that teenagers are at the bottom of the food chain. The only ones they have authority over are younger siblings and the dog. But then one day that control is lifted, and they find themselves with greater privileges and freedoms because they are adults. Life in Christ means that we are sons of God, adopted into His family because of God's love. Children have all the privileges of being part of a family, and it is the same when we are part of God's family. A son in the New Testament was given a signet ring with the family symbol on it, which offered him the same authority as his father. The Holy Spirit (v. 6) is our signet ring from God.

List two privileges and responsibilities from Scripture we have as children of God. What privilege or responsibility will you claim today?

Thursday · GALATIANS 4:8-18

DIGGING DEEPER • When teenagers learn to drive, there is a ton of stuff to remember. There are things they are supposed to do, things they are not supposed to do, and they have to remember all of it within a moment's notice—sometimes just to drive safely. In today's passage, Paul reminded the Gentiles in Galatia of the basics of being a Christian: 1) Don't be in bondage as slaves to idols or demons or other men (*those which are by nature not gods*–v. 8); 2) Know God and thereby serve Him (v. 9); 3) Don't turn to those who are weak and who do not really work (v. 9b –The Galatians had turned to Jewish traditions instead of God's Word, and it did not work); 4) Return to doing what is good and be passionate about it (v. 18).

List two things that most often cause you to be distracted from doing what you should for the Lord. Why? What will you do to change that?

Friday · GALATIANS 4:19-26

Q

A

DIGGING DEEPER • Remember when you tried to give advice or made a suggestion and someone responded with "You're not my mother!", or, "Who died and left you in charge?" Too often, we want to run our own lives according to our own plans, and we see help from others as interference. Paul is asking the Christians in Galatia why they are not satisfied with God's promises, but instead seek after the inferior teachings of men. He uses the illustration of Abraham, who would not wait for God to fulfill His promise of giving him a child (i.e., Isaac). Instead, he had a child through another woman, hoping that would be okay. Abraham created a mess because he would not trust God, and the Galatians were doing the same.

Name an area of your life, such as friends or free time, in which you have taken control from God. Pray and take the right steps to give it back to Him.

Saturday · GALATIANS 4:27-5:1

Q

A

DIGGING DEEPER • Paul is building on his contrast between *freedom* and *bondage*. Just as Isaac was the *child of promise* to Abraham and Sarah, so those who trust in Christ by faith are also the *children of promise*. As such, *all* (4:26) people of *faith* are *free* a) from bondage to paganism (4:8), b) from bondage to Jewish legalism (4:5), and c) from any other teaching that seeks to draw those of faith back into the *yoke* of works (5:1) to earn salvation. This point is illustrated by the truth that "he who is a slave to the compass has the freedom of the seas." A sailor with compass in hand has freedom to travel the globe, but without that compass he is just lost. A slave to God's promises has freedom from sin's bondage.

List three areas of life in which you are free from fear because you live by the promises of God's word.

QuietTime

WEEK 43

Remember when you have seen in the news that someone has accomplished some great feat and been rewarded for his effort? It is different when a team of people achieve a common goal, because all share in the triumph. This week we learn that believers in the Spirit serve God best when we do it together.

Prayer focus for this week

THE QUESTION · THE ANSWER

What is the writer saying?
How Can I apply this to my life?

Sunday · GALATIANS 5:2-6

Q

A

DIGGING DEEPER · *Good, better, best; never let it rest; until your good is better; and your better is the best.* These are words our parents, teachers, and coaches use to push us beyond mediocrity toward excellence. Paul reminds the church that even though circumcision was good (everything God establishes is good) because it identified the Jewish people as God's chosen ones, it was not more important than faith in Christ. The Jewish Law was given by God at a time in history when He wanted to direct His people toward righteousness and remind them that their salvation was not in keeping the Law, but through forgiveness. The true basis for salvation is found in verse 5: (a) *through the Spirit*, (b) *by faith*, and (c) *wait for the hope of righteousness*. No personal works are mixed in-it's only through faith in Christ.

Name an area that needs improving when it comes to your service for Him.

Monday · GALATIANS 5:7-15

Q

A

DIGGING DEEPER • Have you ever seen someone in the Olympics or at a track meet run into another runner, tripping him and knocking him off course? That is the picture Paul paints when he asks, *Who hindered you from obeying the truth?* The false teachers had tried to trip them up in their understanding of God's Word, and Paul was bringing that to their attention. Like every good coach, Paul reminded them of their past success and of his confidence that they would again succeed. In order to run well they were to (a) *serve one another* (v. 13), (b) *love their neighbors* (v. 14), (c) *take heed* to their conduct (v. 15), (d) *walk* (v. 16) and *live* (v. 25) *in the Spirit* (tomorrow's study), and (e) *desire humility* (v. 26).

List three reasons why you think people have a hard time believing the truth of Scripture. In what area has someone tried to trip you up?

Tuesday · GALATIANS 5:16-21

Q

A

DIGGING DEEPER • Have you ever played or watched someone play a video game in which you can drive different kinds of vehicles through city streets while being chased? It is fun to watch the vehicles crash into buildings, or go over a bridge, or drive through the city park, because the person playing can't steer. Fortunately it is not like that in real life. We have boundaries in which we need to drive. The same is true of our spiritual walk. We can walk in the Spirit by staying within the guidelines of Scripture, or we can walk in our flesh and allow our sinful nature to control our actions and attitudes. Today's passage includes a lengthy list of long words that are important for us to understand so we can avoid sin against God.

Find a commentary or use a different translation of the Bible to help you understand these words, and list beside them what they mean.

Wednesday · GALATIANS 5:22-26

Q

A

DIGGING DEEPER • Remember when you had an opportunity to pick fruit from a tree, or strawberries off the plant? It was no surprise that you found apples on a tree or berries on the plant! Good healthy trees and plants produce the fruit after their kind. Imagine how peculiar (and dangerous) it would be if watermelons were to grow on trees! Today's passage is a reminder that there is evidence of what is going on in our hearts and minds by the *fruit* we produce in our spiritual lives. When we read the list in today's passage, we understand that our lives are to reflect Christ and what He has to offer people. The purpose for having these characteristics in our lives is to use them for God's glory as we serve others.

Which fruit of the Spirit do you find easiest to produce, and why? Which is the hardest for you, and why? Do others see this fruit in you?

Thursday · GALATIANS 6:1-5

Q

A

DIGGING DEEPER • Paul tells us that we are responsible to help those who are *being overtaken in a fault* (v. 1). *Overtaken* means *drawn into a trap and taken*. It is coupled with *fault* (to misplace one's step; to slip and fall). Thus, Paul gives a picture of a brother who *falls* into the mud of sin because he is careless, not having considered his *steps* that led him into the *trap*. A *spiritual* Christian (one being led by the Spirit and who is growing) shouldn't say, "Well, it is his own fault, let him suffer! Maybe next time he will be more careful." While such a comment may be true, it is not very loving. Love demands that the *spiritual* one come to the aid of the *overtaken* and *restore* him.

Why is it so hard for us to restore fellow Christians who find themselves in sinful behavior? Why should we help in any way we can?

Friday · GALATIANS 6:6-10

Q

A

DIGGING DEEPER •   It is always good to know the rules, because then we can prepare. If you get caught driving without your seat belt, the rule is that you will get a ticket. If you jump in the lake with big rocks in your pockets and no life jacket, you will sink and drown. If you plant watermelon seeds, you will get watermelons. Again today, we learn a biblical life principle illustrated by a common occurrence. When we set our hearts, minds, and wills to be a servant of our flesh, we will reap corruption. Paul once again encourages his readers by reminding them that if they do not get tired of doing good deeds they will reap good fruit instead of works of the flesh. The best way to fight the good fight is with the help of others.

Who is the person you depend on to help you develop the fruit of the Spirit? Ask him or her to hold you accountable for one specific area today.

Saturday · GALATIANS 6:11-18

Q

A

DIGGING DEEPER •   To stress importance, Paul takes the pen from his scribe and writes this last paragraph with bold letters. The three sections of the conclusion correspond, in reverse order, to the three sections of the letter. *First*, he warns that the false teachers, who were *constraining* (v. 12b) the Galatians to be *circumcised*, were not interested in the spiritual welfare of the Galatians. *Second*, Paul makes a final defense of his own credentials. *Third*, Paul says he has *marks* (v. 17b) on his body to prove that his arguments in this letter are true. Paul loved his brothers in Christ. This was what motivated him to reprove, encourage, and instruct them concerning their walk with Christ.

List two reasons that it is important to help our friends with their Christian walks, even when it means confronting their sin.

QuietTime

WEEK 44

Everybody is looking for the "good life." What does it take to stay on top? This week we get a good dose of advice from the wisest man who ever lived—Solomon. He shares what we need to understand and do in order to experience the "good life."

Prayer focus for this week

THE **QUESTION** *What is the writer saying?*
THE **ANSWER** *How Can I apply this to my life?*

Sunday · PROVERBS 11:1-11

DIGGING DEEPER • These verses contrast two distinct lifestyles: 1) the person of honesty, wisdom, and righteousness, and 2) the dishonest, prideful, and wicked person. Dishonesty, pride, and wickedness lead a person into a life pitted against God. Whenever man pits himself against God, man loses. Honesty, wisdom, and righteousness lead a person into a lifestyle glorifying to God. The consequences are emphasized. The Lord hates dishonesty. Pride brings shame, perverseness destroys, and money is worthless at death. The wicked trip over their sins and fall, but God delights in truthfulness. Integrity guides. A good person has direction in life. Wisdom and righteousness in an individual not only bring peace and blessing to him, but also to everyone around him—family, church, and community. **Which lifestyle is wiser? Is it a good idea to choose a bad life? Why?**

Monday · PROVERBS 11:12-21

Q

A

DIGGING DEEPER · This section continues the contrasts and consequences of a God-honoring lifestyle compared to an ungodly one. Honoring God in life brings honor to a person and causes that person to treat others honorably as well. Examples: wisdom dictates overlooking and keeping quiet about other people's failures (vv. 12-13); virtue becomes its own reward (vv. 17a, 18b); the upright see life and goodness for themselves (vv. 19a, 21b). However, the ungodly find a different "dishonorable discharge." Examples: fools divulge confidences (vv. 12-13); with no godly counsel, people fall (v. 14); evildoers have multiplied problems (vv. 17b, 19b). Though they join up in gangs to protect themselves, the wicked WILL BE punished (v. 21a).
How can you honor God in your life? How can you treat others honorably?

Tuesday · PROVERBS 11:22-31

Q

A

DIGGING DEEPER · "Word pictures" communicate so much. Verse 22 is an interesting mental image. The value of having virtue and wisdom far exceeds that of being beautiful, popular, or rich. Beauty, popularity, and riches are worthless commodities in eternity. Those who grasp for these earthly things sadly find themselves with empty hands and empty hearts. There is an unalterable law in God's creation (vv. 25, 31): "You reap what you sow," or, in modern terms, "What goes around, comes around." Plant a life of mischief and evil, and mischief and evil will boomerang back into your life. But plant a life of righteousness and good, win souls to God, follow hard after the will of the Lord, and you will find God's rewards both in this life and in the life to come.
Are earthly things or spiritual things of more value? Why do you win souls?

Wednesday · PROVERBS 12:1-10

Q

A

DIGGING DEEPER · Being *teachable* yields the favor of both God and man. A pliable spirit, willing to receive correction, rebuke, and exhortation, is a personality trait that comes easily to some, but requires work for others. It is worth it, because loving instruction and being taught of the Lord is pleasing to God. The instruction manual for life—the Bible-teaches right from wrong in every relationship, from husband and wife to best friends. Taught by the Scriptures, a righteous man will not be moved, and a righteous woman will be the pride of her husband. The truth will stand, while lies will wrap themselves around the legs of the liar and cause his downfall. A *perverse heart* (v. 8) is morally crooked, and refuses to be straightened out by being taught the good and the right way.

What does it mean to be teachable? How is being teachable profitable?

Thursday · PROVERBS 12:11-19

Q

A

DIGGING DEEPER · After a quick reminder that hard work is rewarded with bread on the table, and that it is a waste to hang out with unsavory characters, this passage focuses on talking and listening. Most people have felt the satisfaction in knowing they said the right thing at the right time, and in the right way. It's a good feeling. Likewise, most people have felt the sense of sorrow caused when words were used like a knife to cut them down and carve them up. It leaves a bad feeling. The wise learn how to use their tongues to build up. Fools speak in negatives and profanities, using their mouths to tear down. Being true and speaking truthfully will stand forever, because truth is based in the very nature of God. Verbal abuse is real and hurts. On the flip side, kind words are incredibly powerful to lift others up.

Why are words so influential? How can you be wise in word choices?

Friday · PROVERBS 12:20-28

Q

A

DIGGING DEEPER • The evaluation of life hinges on two things: words and actions. What we say and what we do are a direct reflection of who we are and what we believe. Our words and actions divulge so much about us. That's why it is so easy to recognize a fool. He babbles foolishness, and he acts foolishly (v. 23b). A fool is lazy, does not enjoy work, whines and complains the whole time, ends up at the bottom of the stack, and, by using people, brings upon himself the disdain of others. A man of wisdom, however, works hard, lives good days, keeps confidences, is a delight to the Lord, a leader, a blessing to others, and is filled with joy. He knows how to say a good word. What a welcome addition he is to a growing, peaceful society.

What are some of the things you say and do when the circumstances of your life are good? When they are bad? What does this say about you?

Saturday · PROVERBS 13:1-13

Q

A

DIGGING DEEPER • Listening to and obeying parents is sometimes a chore. It seems like they have no understanding of the "real" and "important" issues of life. At times it may be a chore, but wise children do give heed to their parents. Obeying parents when we are young trains our souls to obey God when we are adults. That's why the Bible makes such a big deal about obedience. How we start out is often how we end up. Ignoring godly instruction will make our life *loathsome* (v. 5), which means, foul-smelling. On the other hand, when we learn (memorize) the commandments and obey them, we are made rich, no matter what our bank balance. Obedience results in an uplifted life. Disobedience results in a downtrodden life. Pride keeps us from obeying (v. 10). Conforming to God's Word yields great reward.

What difference does it make to be obedient? Why does it seem so hard?

QuietTime

WEEK 45

Have you ever made a really bad move or decision that cost you the game, or worse, maybe a friendship? In the coming week we are going to see how to avoid "bad moves." As you read, see if you can pick up some tips on "good moves."

Prayer focus for this week

THE QUESTION *What is the writer saying?*
THE ANSWER *How Can I apply this to my life?*

Sunday · PROVERBS 13:14-25

DIGGING DEEPER • The *fountain of life* is the Word of God, and obedience to it keeps us from an early grave. There is pleasure in sin for a season, but a heavy price is paid for years of drugs, alcohol, illicit sex, and ungodliness. A *hard* (v. 15) life, calloused by long-term sin, blinds the sinner from seeing the foolishness of his evil ways. "Play hard; die young" is the world's rule. The wise and righteous, though, are willing to accept correction, believe the Word, and honor God. They are rewarded with success (not necessarily materially), long life, and honor. Our friends and peers have much to do with our choice of path (v. 20). The wages of sin is death, but to the righteous, good shall be repaid. Parents who love us enough to instruct us, correct us, and even discipline us, do us a favor. **What choices will ensure that you stay on the right path? Make them today.**

Monday · PROVERBS 14:1-12

Q
A

DIGGING DEEPER • Life can be reduced to our choices—what we choose to believe, with whom we choose to associate, etc. Arrogant people boldly speak against the Lord, His servants, and His ways. They fail to realize that the "good life" requires a choice to invest faith, time, talent, and treasure in the things of God. Habitual choices mold our future. What we choose today determines what we are tomorrow. A *scorner* is a borderline fool. He has listened to fools and chosen poorly for so long, he fails to recognize wisdom even when he trips over it. A wise son knows the influence of friends, so he limits his interaction with fools and scorners. Fools make the righteous feel foolish for being good, but in the end the righteous win. *Intermeddle* means *to share*. Consequences of our choices are ours alone.
How can you be sure your choices are right? Is it wise to hang with fools?

Tuesday · PROVERBS 14:13-23

Q
A

DIGGING DEEPER • Sometimes we can be laughing on the outside, but cold and lonely on the inside. Most of the time a distance between us and God causes this condition. The *backslider* is a person who is morally undeveloped. Backsliders have "sour lives" in order to show them that it is better to stay close to God. The wise consider the consequences of their actions before acting. They have good, clean fun. Fools act impulsively and, many times, are public jerks. Eventually, in this life or the next, the wicked will be forced to acknowledge that "being good in God is the best life." Talk is cheap (v. 23), and nothing is gained by it. However, working hard and serving the Lord is profitable, rewarding, and satisfying both in this life and in the life to come.
Why is it so easy to leap before you look? How can you change that?

Wednesday · Proverbs 14:24-35

DIGGING DEEPER · The wise handle their finances shrewdly. Money spent on sinful pleasures is gone. The truth sets free, while deceivers speak lies. To have the *fear of the Lord* means to reverence and acknowledge God and His authority over our lives. This attitude toward God initiates us into wisdom, which protects us and nourishes our souls. An angry person speaks in the rush of emotion and often spouts words he later severely regrets. Wisdom bites the tongue and tries to understand before speaking out. A *sound heart* refers to a heart at peace with itself, others, and God. This is priceless. "Green with envy" means "sick with jealousy"—desiring what others have, or, on the flip side, destroying something that we can't have so that no one else can have it, either. **What are ways you fear the Lord? How do you strive for a sound heart?**

Thursday · Proverbs 15:1-11

DIGGING DEEPER · Yell in anger at someone who is yelling angrily at you, and you will get nothing but angry yelling and no solutions. The quiet, steady approach quells the beast of anger. Nothing thought, done, or said is hidden from the Lord—nothing. Remembering this should spur us toward good. *Breach* means *to tear*. Our tongues can either tear down the spirits or lift up and inspire the souls of others. Fools reject their parents' guidance. Wisdom reveres father and mother. The fool is all take and no give. The ungodly try to sacrifice for God and will be rejected, but the Lord delights in the words spoken to Him by the righteous. *Abomination* is something disgusting to God—illicit sex, idolatry, and immorality. God knows our hearts. **What is the best way to resolve an angry argument? Why do you think that is? How can you have the respect of God so He delights to hear your words?**

Friday · PROVERBS 15:12-22

DIGGING DEEPER • In Proverbs, a *fool* is not someone with a mental deficiency. *Fool* more accurately refers to the morally or biblically deficient person who has rejected God's Word. A fool is "in your face" when corrected by the wise. Our heart attitude directly affects our mental and emotional well-being. God and His Word can change our heart attitude. Both righteousness and foolishness are self-reinforcing. The longer we go in either direction, the stronger the pull to keep going in that direction. Having joy in life does not have to include lots of "things." Take advice from many counselors. Have a teachable spirit, and it will amaze you what God is able to teach you.

What is your reaction when corrected? How does your heart attitude need to be changed? Work on changing it today.

Saturday · PROVERBS 15:23-33

DIGGING DEEPER • To say the right word at the right time, in the right way, is wisdom. It can change the destiny of whole nations, let alone (affect) our friends and family. Wisdom results in an enriched long life. The proud rich man will be brought low, while the righteous widow will be protected by the Lord. The thoughts of the wicked disgust God, but He savors the words of the pure. Listening to a righteous man's words transforms us into doing what is right. It's a matter of fearing the Lord and humbling ourselves. The wise revere God, not themselves. They submit to God's way, not their own; they allow wise men to guide, and do not "go it alone"; and seek to give more than to receive.

How can you train your mind to be able to say the right things? How do wisdom and righteousness interlock to produce a God-pleasing life?

QuietTime

WEEK 46

Have you ever been a part of a church that seemed like one big family? Maybe you're a part of that kind of church right now. Paul and his friends loved the church in Thessalonica...just like family.

Prayer focus for this week

THE QUESTION *What is the writer saying?*
THE ANSWER *How Can I apply this to my life?*

Sunday · 1 Thessalonians 1:1-5

DIGGING DEEPER · Isn't it nice to hear someone say "Thank you"? We all welcome it when people express their appreciation for something we've done. God values our expressions of thanks as well. We should routinely give thanks for such things as meals, family members, and learning opportunities. When was the last time you expressed thanks to God for your church? Paul, Silas, and Timothy together send this letter to the church they started in Thessalonica to let them know how thankful they were for them, and how often they prayed for them. Each of their names has significant meaning and indicates qualities we should incorporate into our lives.

Who can you say "thank you" to today? When was the last time you thanked God for your church? What are some ways you can do it?

Monday · 1 THESSALONIANS 1:6-10

Q

A

DIGGING DEEPER • One of the main problems in the church today is similar to that of the early church: believers were being ostracized for their faith. What a shame! The Christians in the church in Thessalonica give us a good description of what Christians should look like. In our passage today, we specifically see that the Christians in this church maintained an attitude of joy despite persecution (v. 6), consistently lived the Christian life in their community (v. 7), shared their faith in their city and beyond (v. 8), and testified of how the Lord had changed their lives (v. 9). This is a great model for us to follow as we serve the Lord in our own local church.

How would Paul, Silas, and Timothy describe your church? Would they brag about you or be disappointed? How can you make a difference?

Tuesday · 1 THESSALONIANS 2:1-8

Q

A

DIGGING DEEPER • Have you ever met someone you didn't trust? We all have. There have always been people in this world who are untrustworthy. Even in the first century, there were those who ran scams and tried to take advantage of people. Evidently, some people thought that Paul might be untrustworthy. So he made it absolutely clear that he was more than trustworthy by reminding the skeptics that he had *suffered* for his efforts to share the Gospel (v. 2). He also made it clear that his preaching did not contain any *deceit* (v. 3), nor did it contain any sort of *flattering words* (v. 5). He was honest and truthful in all areas of his life, and his lifestyle and words were proof of that.

What does your lifestyle say about you? Do people think you're honest? Does God think you are honest?

Wednesday · 1 THESSALONIANS 2:9-13

DIGGING DEEPER •   Imagine for a minute that you were called to a witness stand and challenged by a prosecutor to vouch for your best friend's spiritual life. Could you defend that person? Would it be difficult for you to honestly compliment his spiritual life, or would you have to plead the Fifth Amendment and not say anything at all? When it comes to the Christian life, it's so important that what we say is backed up by how we live. The saying and doing should be the same. Paul and his companions are so confident in their testimony that they call the whole church in Thessalonica as *witnesses* to the fact that they are the real deal. What they saw is what they got.

Could your friends vouch for your Christian life? Could they stand up in front of others and honestly say you are the real deal?

Thursday · 1 THESSALONIANS 2:14-20

DIGGING DEEPER •   Have you ever really missed someone? Maybe you missed a friend or family member and couldn't wait to see him, embrace him, or hear his voice. When we recall all the fond memories and shared blessings, it causes us to want to get together with fellow believers as often as we can. Paul felt the same way about this church in Thessalonica. He loved them so much. He saw them as family, and he had a *great desire* to see them in person (v. 17). He really missed being around them, and he couldn't wait for an opportunity to see them again. But be aware that we have an enemy who wants to hinder any such times of fellowship. "Divide and conquer" is his familiar strategy.

When you're out of town, do you miss your church family? What is it about being with them that brings you joy and fulfillment?

Friday · 1 Thessalonians 3:1-5

Q

A

DIGGING DEEPER • Christians aren't immune from trouble. We have problems just like everyone else. In fact, it can probably be argued that we have more problems than the unsaved. Paul says in his particular situation that he was *appointed* for these problems (v. 3). Evidently, Paul had alerted the believers in Thessalonica to expect a certain amount of persecution, and, in fact, it had already happened (v. 4). If our Lord experienced misunderstanding and persecution, should we expect anything different? On the contrary, we should expect a certain amount of persecution for our faith, and recognize it as an opportunity to grow in our relationship with God. Had any persecution lately?

What can we learn from the various troubles and problems that we experience in our lives? How should we react when they come?

Saturday · 1 Thessalonians 3:6-13

Q

A

DIGGING DEEPER • Do you have any friends in other parts of the world? You probably love to hear how your friends are doing, and especially how they are growing in their relationships with God. Paul had many friends all over the world in his day too, and some of them were in this church in Thessalonica. He loved to hear how they were doing, and how they were growing in their relationships with God. He couldn't always say that about some other churches. Good news always makes one glad. In this passage, Paul tells his friends how excited he is to hear that they are growing in the Lord and are well.

What friends can you call or e-mail today to check on how they're doing in their Christian life? Why not give them a call and offer words of encouragement? Who is first on your list? When will you call them?

QuietTime

As Paul finishes his letter, he comments on an assortment of topics, ranging from holy living to the Rapture of the Church, to church relationships, and even the basics of Christian living. What a combination!

Prayer focus for this week

THE QUESTION *What is the writer saying?*
THE ANSWER *How Can I apply this to my life?*

Sunday · 1 THESSALONIANS 4:1-8

DIGGING DEEPER · God is all about holiness. First and foremost, He is holy, perfect, and without sin. But more than that, His will for our lives is that we be holy, too. The biblical word for this is *sanctification* (v. 3). As Christians, we have a responsibility to live holy lives because it is *the will of God* (v. 3). This takes time and we may suffer a few setbacks, but the important thing is that we are steadily growing. Specifically in this passage, Paul wants us to be holy in the area of sexual purity. He knows we have problems with our thought life and they can carry over into our behavior. He comments on this by saying that God has *not called us unto uncleanness, but unto holiness* (v. 7).

What are some hindrances to holiness? Is my relationship with the Lord and others holy and healthy?

Monday · 1 THESSALONIANS 4:9-12

Q

A

DIGGING DEEPER • What do you think most churches in America are known for today? Are they known for their buildings, size, problems, or even their pastors? Have you ever heard of a church that was known for its love? The church in Thessalonica had this reputation. In fact, this church was so skilled at loving others, Paul told them that he didn't even need to address that area of their lives, because they had been *taught of God to love one another* (v. 9). Wouldn't it be great to be part of a church where loving relationships are abundant, rather than fighting and squabbling over a lot of non-essentials?

What do you think most churches in America are known for? What are you doing in your church that will make it more like the church in Thessalonica? Where will you begin, and whom will it involve?

Tuesday · 1 THESSALONIANS 4:13-18

Q

A

DIGGING DEEPER • What happens to believers who die before Jesus comes back? This may not be an important question to you, but what if you were a new believer in Thessalonica and some of your loved ones had already died? It would be a biggie! Paul gives them the answer by saying that those who die before Jesus returns at the Rapture will not miss out, but will instead experience the event in a different way. Paul says, *the dead in Christ shall rise first* (v. 16), meaning they're going to lead the way! Other believers will join them. What a reunion! If you think it doesn't get any better than this, just wait!

What would you like to be caught doing when Christ returns? He's coming again; are you ready? He's saying, "Ready or not, here I come!"

Wednesday · 1 THESSALONIANS 5:1-8

DIGGING DEEPER • Have you ever read various statements in the Bible and wondered what in the world they mean? We all have. Maybe you've wondered about the recurring phrase that says *the day of the Lord* (v. 2), and are not sure of its meaning. Our curiosity indicator rises to a new high when we see several of these statements and do not have any answers. You might even be saying, "What is *the day of the Lord*? When does it happen?" and "Where does it happen?" You are not the first to think or ask these questions. The answer in a nutshell is this: *the day of the Lord* is a time in the future where God judges the wicked. It's for unbelievers, and there will be no escape or excuse. **What are you doing to warn people of the Day of the Lord? Are you sharing the Good News (the alternative to this bad news) with others?**

Thursday · 1 THESSALONIANS 5:9-15

DIGGING DEEPER • What does a pastor do? Does he do anything besides preach and take up the offering? Does he just read his Bible all day, or what? Have you ever asked yourself those kinds of questions? The truth is, pastors are perhaps the busiest people on this planet. In this section of Scripture, Paul takes a little time to let us know that pastors work hard, and that the church's responsibility is *to esteem them very highly in love for their work's sake* (v. 13). They deserve our respect in that they not only work hard, but they carry a great deal of responsibility, overseeing the work of the local church as well as ministering in many people's lives...including yours! **Do you pray for your pastor? How could you encourage your pastor this week?**

Friday · 1 Thessalonians 5:16-22

DIGGING DEEPER • If you think you can't memorize Scripture, try some of our verses today. Paul gives us several simple truths to think about and work on. He tells us to *rejoice evermore* (v. 16), which means we should always be joyful. He encourages us to *pray without ceasing* (v. 17), which doesn't mean to pray non-stop, but, instead, to remain in a constant attitude of prayer, praying regularly and persistently. *In every thing give thanks* (v. 18) is obvious, but notice it says *in* everything and not *for* everything. Paul gives us several other short admonitions as well. These all provide us with some important principles upon which we can grow spiritually. **How are you doing in the joy department? How's your prayer life? Are you giving thanks in everything?**

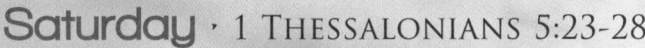

Saturday · 1 Thessalonians 5:23-28

DIGGING DEEPER • God is faithful. He's faithful in little things and big things. You can count on Him in every aspect of your life. He is so much more reliable than anyone else in your life. While everyone around you fails or disappoints you at one time or another, He continues to be faithful. In spite of our own times of unfaithfulness, His faithfulness abounds still. Every second of every minute of every hour of every day of every year God remains *faithful* (v. 24), and He doesn't break promises or fail to come through for us. That's more than anyone else can or ever will be able to do. What a faithful God we serve! **How has God been faithful to you? How have you shown your faithfulness? Why not begin with one of the following: Prayer, Bible Reading, Scripture Memory, Faithful Attendance, or Witnessing?**

QuietTime

WEEK 48

It's always great to hear from old friends. This week, Paul again writes to his friends in Thessalonica, and instructs and encourages them. As we read this letter, may we be just as blessed and encouraged as they were.

Prayer focus for this week

THE QUESTION — *What is the writer saying?*
THE ANSWER — *How Can I apply this to my life?*

Sunday · 2 Thessalonians 1:1-5

Q

A

DIGGING DEEPER · Have you ever felt like saying "thank you" to someone who followed Jesus so closely it made a difference in your life? Paul did. In fact, Paul commends not just one believer, but the entire church of Thessalonica! They were growing in their relationships with God (vertically) as evidenced by their *faith* (v. 3), and they were growing in their relationships with others (horizontally), as evidenced by their *charity* (v. 3), or love. On top of that, they were doing it in the face of persecution! No wonder Paul is so proud of them. What a role model for us to follow! We all need to have that kind of Christianity. It's real!

Are you growing in your relationship with God? What about your relationship with others? Does it need to improve today? What will you do to make a change? What kind of a role model are you?

Monday · 2 THESSALONIANS 1:6-12

Q

A

DIGGING DEEPER • What do you think of when you hear the phrase *everlasting destruction*? You probably didn't think immediately of warm, fuzzy kittens. And you shouldn't, because according to verse 9, it's a phrase that describes Hell itself. It is a place reserved for those who don't know God, and never really wanted to know Him. It's not pleasant to think that a place like this really exists. It's uncomfortable for us to talk about, sometimes even in church. Very few sermons are preached on Hell. But the truth is, Hell is a real place, reserved for real people who have rejected a real God and His offer of a real personal relationship with Jesus Christ...and their punishment will also be very real!

To whom can you witness this week so that they do not have to experience that everlasting destruction someday?

Tuesday · 2 THESSALONIANS 2:1-5

Q

A

DIGGING DEEPER • Has anyone ever given you a nickname? Did you like it? How would you like the nickname *man of sin*? Not the coolest nickname ever, huh? This is certainly one title nobody would covet. And yet, this is the nickname given to the man more commonly known as the Antichrist. In case you're unfamiliar with this person, the best way to describe him is a man whose purpose is to deceive the nations into following his leadership and worshiping him as god. He will begin his work when all of the Christians are taken away at the Rapture, and will be defeated when Jesus Christ returns again.

Why do you think so many people will follow the leadership of the Antichrist? What can you do to prevent people from listening and following him? Can you think of someone in need? Start today!

Wednesday · 2 Thessalonians 2:6-12

DIGGING DEEPER · Have you ever played with puppets? You have probably at least put a sock on your hand and imagined it as a character of some sort. Anyway, as you use a puppet (or sock), you determine everything that puppet says and does. You determine its personality, its voice, and its mannerisms. Everything. You control it completely. The Antichrist, whom we see once again in our verses today, is nothing but a puppet. He is controlled by Satan himself. Satan/the Devil is the real mastermind behind all the chaos, confusion, and conflict. Knowing his time is short, his ultimate goal is to ruin as many lives as he can and get as many following him as possible.

Do you think Satan is working in the world today? How is he working? What can you do to thwart his efforts? How will you start?

Thursday · 2 Thessalonians 2:13-17

DIGGING DEEPER · How are you feeling right now? Are you exhausted from a busy day? Upset because of a huge argument with your parents? Lonely because you've just moved to a new place? However you're feeling right now as you read these words, be encouraged. Our God loves you. He cares about you. He has your best interests in mind. So, instead of being down, let Him *comfort* your heart (v. 17). And more than that, let Him *stablish* (establish) *you in every good word and work* (v. 17), which basically means to let Him give you His strength. God cares about you. Be comforted and strengthened. The hymn writer said it correctly in the song, *What a Friend We Have in Jesus.*

What is keeping you from experiencing the Lord's comfort? Are you taking Him up on the offer of His strength?

Friday · 2 Thessalonians 3:1-5

DIGGING DEEPER • The Lord is faithful. That's such a brief statement, and it may seem overused, but for many of us, there aren't a whole lot of things that we can count on. Friends have let us down, family members have disappointed us, and even church members have not been there when we needed them. To be fair, we've let people down ourselves, too. But the Lord has never let anyone down. He is faithful. He was faithful when Paul wrote this letter, and He is faithful as we read these Bible verses and even this brief thought. The Lord is faithful! There's nothing you will need that He cannot and will not provide. If you want to be kept from evil, learn to trust Him.

How has God shown Himself to be faithful in your life? Aren't you glad that you can count on Him never to fail you? Trust Him today.

Saturday · 2 Thessalonians 3:6-18

DIGGING DEEPER • Work hard. This short little sentence doesn't seem like it needs much explanation, does it? But evidently, a certain number of Christians in the church of Thessalonica didn't get it. It seems that, for some reason, they didn't feel like they needed to work at all, much less work hard. Paul takes the lead in this situation and commands them to begin working and to work hard. Today there seems to be a mind-set that the world and the church owe us something. Rather than thinking, "What can the church do for me," ask yourself, "What can I do for the Lord and the church?"

Should you work hard in whatever situation you're in? Are you doing your part at home to help out? How about at church?

QuietTime

WEEK 49

Do you want to know what God's will for your life is? Pay close attention and you could find out this week. Have you ever gone on a treasure hunt? This week we'll find out what Paul considered to be the greatest treasure of all.

Prayer focus for this week

THE QUESTION
THE ANSWER

What is the writer saying?
How Can I apply this to my life?

Sunday · COLOSSIANS 1:1-8

Q
A

DIGGING DEEPER · Have you ever asked yourself "Who am I?" or, "Why am I here?" These are questions we all ask ourselves. Paul addresses this letter to the "saints." When we are *in Christ* through the forgiveness of our sins, we become *saints* positionally. We may not always act like it in everyday life, but that is who we are in Christ. Paul was impressed and thankful for the faith, hope, and love of the Colossian believers. They responded quickly to the Gospel and worked hard to bear fruit in their lives.

Are you a saint? Are you set apart? Do your friends see faith, hope, and love exhibited in your life? Make a list of at least three things that you are in Christ and three reasons you are here for Him.

Monday · COLOSSIANS 1:9-14

Q

A

DIGGING DEEPER • Do you want to know God's will for your life? Where you should go to school or whom to marry may not be specifically answered by a verse, but you can know God well enough to know His desires. Paul tells us that to know God's will for our lives and to gain wisdom, we must know His Word. You will see four important results in your life as you get closer to God through daily Bible study. First, you will begin to constantly bear fruit. Secondly, you will begin to regularly grow in the knowledge of God and in fellowship with Him. Third, you will be strengthened by His power. And fourth, you will develop a thankful spirit for all that He does.
Ask God to reveal His will to you in a specific area as you spend time in His Word this week. Does your life exhibit these four results of spending time in His Word?

Tuesday · COLOSSIANS 1:15-19

Q

A

DIGGING DEEPER • What sets Christianity apart from all the other religions of the world? It is the fact that Jesus Christ is God. Theologians call it the doctrine of the Deity of Christ. This means that Jesus claimed to be, and is, 100% God. Paul teaches us in verse 15 that Jesus Christ is the *firstborn* of God the Father. *Firstborn* here does not mean *sequence* but *position* and *authority*. He is supreme in the universe and in the church. He is also over all creation, because He is the one who created all things. With that being true, then the argument that He was created is shattered and can't possibly be true. He is eternal and holds the universe together. What a claim! No wonder many religions of the world hate the very mention of His name!
Think seriously about who Jesus Christ is. Compare John 1:1-3 and Hebrews 1:1-3 with today's passage.

Wednesday · COLOSSIANS 1:20-23

Q

A

DIGGING DEEPER • We all once were enemies of God, but when Jesus died on the cross and rose from the dead, He provided a way for us to be reconciled to God. Reconciliation means we can exchange hostility toward God for friendship with Him. Whereas we were once enemies of God, we can now be friends with Him. What Jesus did on the cross is available to the entire world, but it is up to each individual to respond personally to the Gospel. There are still untold millions who have never heard of this great news. God wants to have a loving relationship with them, too, but they must hear and respond favorably to the Gospel in order to experience it.
Have you been reconciled to God by asking Jesus to forgive your sins? Are you holy and blameless and beyond reproach? With whom can you share the good news of reconciliation today?

Thursday · COLOSSIANS 1:24-29

Q

A

DIGGING DEEPER • Do you like to get into a good mystery book or watch a "whodunit" video? Are you ever tempted to go to the end and find out how it ends before finishing? Paul talks about the great mystery that was hidden from the Old Testament saints, but that he was going to reveal to the Colossians. This mystery is Christ's permanent indwelling of every believer—whether Jew or Gentile—by the Holy Spirit. This indwelling is referred to in this passage as *Christ in you*. Christ can now be our *hope of glory*. Paul worked hard and suffered much to share the Gospel everywhere he went. Shouldn't we be willing to do the same?
Meditate on the phrase, Christ in you, the hope of glory. Determine to share this hope with at least one person today.

Friday · COLOSSIANS 2:1-7

Q

A

DIGGING DEEPER · Have you ever gone on a treasure hunt? Maybe at a party you were given a map to figure out where to find the *loot*. Or, did you have to find certain clues and then figure out where the treasure was? It's always fun to discover treasure! Have you ever thought of your personal Bible study as a treasure hunt? That is what Paul is saying in today's passage. He says Jesus Christ is the believer's treasure. In Him is all the wisdom and knowledge we need to be successful in our lives. Daily reading of His Word will produce comfort, cheer, and courage to face each day, and you will enjoy victory like you have never experienced.
Is Jesus Christ your treasure? If not, talk to someone today who can help you find the greatest treasure of all. With whom can you go on a treasure hunt today?

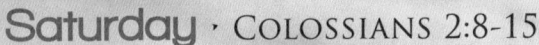

Saturday · COLOSSIANS 2:8-15

Q

A

DIGGING DEEPER · Are you still excited about being on a treasure hunt? Today Paul describes in more exact detail the treasure that we have in Christ. Look closely at all we have *in Him*: In verse 10 we are *complete* in Christ. In verse 11 we are *circumcised* in Him, meaning that at salvation, sin's power over us is removed. In verse 12a we are *buried* with Christ, and in verse 12b, *raised* with Him, meaning that sin no longer has authority over the believer. In verse 13 we are *alive* in Christ. We can experience life the way it was meant to be. In verses 13-14 we are *forgiven* in Christ. In verse 15 we are *triumphant* in Christ. These treasures take on new meaning as they are applied to our lives. As a bonus, they just keep growing!
Think long and hard about who you are in Christ today. What do you need to change in order to live a life worthy of who you are in Christ?

QuietTime

WEEK 50

Who are you in Christ? How do you deal with those in authority over you? Is prayer really important? You'll find the answers to all these questions this week! You'll also discover how important it is both to give and to receive encouragement. Hold on and enjoy your study this week!

Prayer focus for this week

THE QUESTION *What is the writer saying?*
THE ANSWER *How Can I apply this to my life?*

Sunday · COLOSSIANS 2:16-23

Q
A

DIGGING DEEPER • Have you ever felt judged by others? It's not a good feeling, is it? Paul warns us not to allow others to judge our behavior. There are two basic areas that Paul addresses: First is the area of legalism, where the rulers wanted the Christians to continue to obey all the Old Testament laws just so the rulers could have the power instead of giving it over to the Lord Jesus. Our salvation is not something we do, but it's something God has already done! The second area is one we see reemerging today in the worship of angels. Why should we worship created angels when God wants us to worship Him, the Creator of all things? **Are you trying to please the created things (men or angels) or the Creator? Determine to live your life today to please God, not caring what others think.**

Monday · COLOSSIANS 3:1-7

Q

A

DIGGING DEEPER • Who are you *in Christ*? Notice that Paul uses the word *since* in verse 1, not *if* or *when*. This explains that we have been forgiven and are in a new position in Christ. *Since* we have been raised with Christ we are to constantly and habitually seek the things above (v. 2). *Since* you have died to sin and the world (v. 3; Galatians 2:20) you are to live on a higher level with higher expectations. *Since* we are in Christ, we must consider our bodies as dead to earthly passions (v. 5). We need to make daily choices that sometimes go against our fleshly desires but that will help us live on a higher level.

Do something today to show that you are indeed in Christ. Make a decision to show others that you live on a higher level.

Tuesday · COLOSSIANS 3:8-17

Q

A

DIGGING DEEPER • When was the last time you were really filthy dirty? Maybe it was after a long, hot day of work, or after playing soccer, football, or any game in the rain. Whatever it was, you were so glad to get home, shed your dirty clothes, and take a long, refreshing shower. That is how Paul compares our new life in Christ to the old one. Old sin and attitudes are to be put off and new godly ones put on. We are to put on the things listed in verses 12-13, plus love (v. 14) and peace (v. 15). In verse 11 Paul thought it important to point out that after we become Christians, cultural and social distinctions are erased and we are to be one in Christ. As the saying goes, "the ground is level at the foot of the cross."

What godly characteristics do you need to put on in your life? Look at the list in verses 12-15 and pick one to work on specifically today.

Wednesday · Colossians 3:18-4:1

Q

A

DIGGING DEEPER • What do you think our society would look like if everyone followed today's text? It sure would look different, wouldn't it? There is something here for everyone. It is interesting Paul starts with wives, but by using a military term here, he tells women to be *a rank under* their husbands. Husbands are to love their wives and not provoke their children. Children are to obey their parents, a command which has a promise with it (Ephesians 6:3). You may think the slave and master instructions do not apply today, but if you apply them to employees and employers, you can see that they do. Each of us is to work knowing that the Lord is over the other.

Shock your parents or employer today by doing something unexpected. Obey them exactly as told, immediately, and with a good attitude.

Thursday · Colossians 4:2-6

Q

A

DIGGING DEEPER • When was the last time you seriously spent some time in prayer? Paul is telling us that prayer is the essential thing we need as believers to carry out the commands he just gave (yesterday's text). It is only through prayer for each other that we'll see lives changed and our service succeed. We are to pray with an attitude of thanks (v. 2), and for others to be able to share the Gospel clearly (vv. 3-4). Do you remember the mystery Paul is referring to? It is the fact that Jesus indwells every believer in the person of the Holy Spirit. Paul also reminds us of the importance of living a consistent, godly life before unbelievers.

Pray specifically for an opportunity for you or a friend to share the Gospel with someone today! Are you living consistently before others?

Friday · COLOSSIANS 4:7-11

Q
A

DIGGING DEEPER • Did you know that your name is what you like to hear the most? Science has proven that. In today's passage Paul is commending certain people to the Colossians. Tychicus and Onesimus were taking this letter to the Colossians with instructions to tell them all about Paul and his ministry, and to encourage them in the faith. Aristarchus was a fellow prisoner with Paul who had suffered much for the Gospel. It is interesting to see Paul's fond mention of Mark, since the two of them had a falling out earlier in their ministry (Acts 13:13; 15:37-38). Justus also proved to be an encouragement to Paul. Encouragement is one of the best ways to promote harmony and fellowship among believers.
Think of someone you can call by name, and be an encouragement to him or her today. Think of someone else and do it again!

Saturday · COLOSSIANS 4:12-18

Q
A

DIGGING DEEPER • Do you share your letters with those around you? It probably depends on the content. Again, Paul names people and comments on their work for the Gospel. Paul's love and concern for believers from many backgrounds and nationalities is reflected in these words. It is interesting that Paul, a Jew, speaks so highly of Epaphras, a Gentile. He was impressed with the earnest prayer and concern that Epaphras had for the Colossians' spirituality. Dr. Luke and Demas were with Paul and sent greetings. Paul's mention of the Laodiceans shows that the churches had shared their letters with one another. Archippus is charged to be vigilant in the ministry. Paul tells him not to quit—the Christian life is a lifetime commitment.
Put your name in place of Archippus and pretend Paul said these words to you. What should you do differently to cause the ministry to grow?

QuietTime

WEEK 51

Peter will always be known by the church as a man of action. In this letter, you'll see why he earned his reputation as he attacks the false teachers of his day head-on.

Prayer focus for this week

THE QUESTION — *What is the writer saying?*
THE ANSWER — *How Can I apply this to my life?*

Sunday · 2 PETER 1:1-4

Q
A

DIGGING DEEPER • What do you think of when you see or hear the word *powerful*? Some of you probably think of the center of our solar system, the sun. Others might think of Niagara Falls or the white water rapids your youth group recently tried to conquer. Still others might think of electricity. But how many of us would think about Jesus? He is indeed powerful. We don't often describe Jesus as powerful, but Peter lets us know that Jesus is powerful; not only that, but Jesus makes His power available to us as we pursue a holy life. So why not access His power today? Quit trying to live the Christian life in your own strength. Let our *powerful* Savior help you.

Why don't we think of Jesus as powerful? How can you regularly remind yourself that He is powerful and wants to help you?

Monday · 2 PETER 1:5-9

Q

A

DIGGING DEEPER • God expects you to live a certain kind of life! In fact, Peter makes a list of various qualities and characteristics that believers should consider *normal* for their everyday lives. First on the list is *virtue* (v. 5), which is simply moral excellence. God expects us to live morally excellent lives. *Knowledge* (v. 5) comes next and implies that the Christian should be involved in the study of God's Word. *Temperance* (v. 6) follows knowledge. It's a fancy word for self-control. Next comes *patience* (v. 6), or perseverance, and is the ability to continue doing right regardless of one's circumstances. *Godliness* (v. 6) is doing what God says with reverence. And *brotherly kindness* (v. 7) is more than just being nice. It is mutual sacrifice for one another, just like in a family.

How are you doing? Which qualities do you need to work on most?

Tuesday · 2 PETER 1:10-14

Q

A

DIGGING DEEPER • Repetition is the key to learning. Repetition is the key to learning. Repetition is the key to learning. Do you get the point? When teachers repeat something, what are they trying to do? They want to make sure you fully understand what they're saying. If they continue to repeat something over and over again, they want you never to forget it. This is what Peter admits that he's been trying to do. Essentially, he says, "I am going to keep reminding you of the importance of implementing virtue, knowledge, and these other qualities in your lives, even though you already know about them and are putting them into practice." Peter says, "Get it and never forget it!"

Do you get it? How often do you need to be reminded? What two qualities or characteristics will you work on this week?

Wednesday · 2 PETER 1:15-21

Q

A

DIGGING DEEPER • Has anybody ever accused you of believing in fairy tales and fables because you're a Christian? It happens to a lot of us. It has been happening to Christians since the days of the disciples. This is exactly why Peter says of himself and the other early followers of Christ, *we have not followed cunningly devised fables* (v. 16) but we *were eyewitnesses of His majesty*. In a nutshell, Peter says, "We're not making this resurrection thing up. We actually saw Jesus!" History tells us that all these eyewitnesses were so sure that they saw Jesus alive, they were willing to give up their very lives for this belief. Would you die for a fairy tale? **How would you respond to someone who said the Bible was a bunch of stories and fairy tales? What would you be willing to die for?**

Thursday · 2 PETER 2:1-9

Q

A

DIGGING DEEPER • Have you ever seen professional impersonators? It is amazing how well they can imitate people or animals. Maybe you've seen famous people, perhaps even presidents, impersonated. Most of us have seen dozens, if not hundreds, of Elvis impersonators. An impersonator is someone who looks and sounds the same on the outside, but in reality, is completely different. In our passage today, Peter warns of those who impersonate him and others who share the good news. He gives them the labels *false prophets* and *false teachers*, and warns us to watch out for their destructive words and steer clear of their impending doom. **How can you know if someone who claims to be a "Bible teacher" is an impersonator (false teacher) or not?**

Friday · 2 PETER 2:10-16

Q

A

DIGGING DEEPER • If you were to describe your best friend, what kind of words would you use? You would try to be so specific that if someone saw that person on the street they could recognize him. This is exactly what Peter does for us as he describes these false prophets and teachers. He wants us to know them when we see them. He tells us they are *presumptuous* (v. 10), which would indicate arrogance, and self-willed (v. 10), which would tell us they might be stubborn. He goes into great detail about how wicked they are, accusing them of having *eyes full of adultery* (v. 14) and summing it up by saying *they have forsaken the right way* (v. 15). Now you know what to look for!

How would others describe your spiritual life? What kind of adjectives would they use?

Saturday · 2 PETER 2:17-22

Q

A

DIGGING DEEPER • Have you ever been around people who talked and talked—and talked some more? And on top of that, they never really said anything? You may even have someone in mind. Well, this is the description given of false teachers in this section of Scripture. Specifically, Peter says, *they speak great swelling words of vanity* (v. 18), which means they talk a lot, use big words and catchy phrases, but ultimately they say nothing at all. They're full of hot air. How disappointing to hear lots of words but learn nothing at all. People should not only say something; they should have something to say.

Do you know people like this? How should you respond to their teaching? What should you do when it comes to your own words?

There will always be those who oppose Christianity and do their best to change its message. Peter and Jude both understand that, and warn us to avoid the ways of these scoffers and to defend our faith.

Prayer focus for this week

THE QUESTION — *What is the writer saying?*
THE ANSWER — *How Can I apply this to my life?*

Sunday · 2 PETER 3:1-6

DIGGING DEEPER • "I shall return." Maybe at some point in one of your history classes, you ran across that famous quote by General Douglas MacArthur. But did you know that Jesus said it first? Some 2,000 years ago, Jesus promised that He would come back—that He would return for His Church. Yet ever since Jesus left, there have been those who have challenged this truth, saying that He's never coming back. They say things like, "If He's coming, then where is He?" or "What's taking Him so long?" just to stir up trouble. The fact is Jesus is coming back. He will return. It's not a matter of *if*, but *when*. And when He returns, He will come back not as a carpenter, but as a conqueror!

If Jesus were to return for His Church tomorrow, would you be ready? What would you like to be doing when Jesus returns?

Monday · 2 PETER 3:7-12

Q

A

DIGGING DEEPER • God loves people more than anything. That's a fact. He loves us to such an extent that He's delaying Jesus' return to earth so that more people have the ability to respond to His love and enter into a relationship with Him. Specifically, Peter says that God's ultimate desire is that *all should come to repentance* (v. 9). Unfortunately, not all respond positively to God's grace and love. In fact, many people choose to reject His offer of abundant life on earth. Sad to say, but they are also choosing to reject His offer of eternal life in Heaven. If we are interested in the hereafter, remember that the HERE determines the AFTER.
Pray for someone who needs to respond positively to God's invitation of eternal life.

Tuesday · 2 PETER 3:13-18

Q

A

DIGGING DEEPER • When teaching from the Bible, it's always good to conclude with some sort of action step. It's important for people to get up and do something with what they've been taught from God's Word. As Peter finishes up his comments on those who try to distort the Scriptures, he leaves his readers with one final admonition. He says, *Grow in grace, and in the knowledge of our Lord and Saviour Jesus Christ* (v. 18). Peter understands, as should we, that when we pursue spiritual maturity and a better relationship with Jesus, we won't be led astray by false teachers like those he's been referring to throughout his letter. He offers a warning to *beware* and a word of encouragement to *grow*.
Are you making progress in your spiritual life? Are you growing? What can you do today to develop a closer relationship with the Lord?

Wednesday · JUDE 1-7

DIGGING DEEPER • Have you ever started to talk about something, but for some very important reason, you changed the subject? Imagine two friends playing video games together, only to have a rat run across the very floor they're sitting on. Do you think the conversation might change due to the new circumstances? Of course it would! This is what Jude does as he writes this letter (and no, he didn't see a rat!). He wants to write about one subject (salvation), but because of certain circumstances, writes instead about the importance of defending the faith. Specifically, he instructs us to *earnestly contend for the faith* (v. 3), taking a stand against those who wish to twist the Scriptures for their own personal purposes. **What are you doing to defend the faith? What can you do today?**

Thursday · JUDE 8-11

DIGGING DEEPER • If the Bible were still being written today and God chose to comment on your life, what kind of words would He use? We can't be sure of what He would say about us, but we know what He said about three individuals—Cain, Balaam, and Korah. God's words were not in any way complimentary. In fact, each of these men is associated with the most ungodly of men. Scripture tells us about these men so that we can avoid their serious mistakes. You can find Cain's rebellion in Genesis 4:1-15, Balaam's failures in Numbers 22-25, and Korah's ungodliness in Numbers 16:1-35. The end result of their evil choices is like all of those who choose to go against our great God: Divine Judgment.
If the Bible were still being written, what would God say about you?

Friday · JUDE 12-19

Q

A

DIGGING DEEPER • Are you an empty rain cloud? How about a fruitless tree? Could you perhaps be a raging wave? Jude uses these phrases to describe the ungodly. He says the ungodly are clouds *without water* (v. 12), meaning that they look as if they're one thing, but in fact, they're not. When he says they are like trees *without fruit* (v. 12), he instructs us to pay attention to the results of their teaching. Does spiritual growth take place or not? The phrase *raging waves* (v. 13) indicates that they wreak havoc on all they touch. The bottom line is this: the ungodly are dangerous, are given over to sensuality, and do not know the true Spirit of God. **Could you be described as an empty rain cloud, fruitless tree, or raging wave? How would you like God to describe you?**

Saturday · JUDE 20-25

Q

A

DIGGING DEEPER • Are you good at building things? Some people are very skilled at building furniture, houses, bridges, and even skyscrapers. Whether or not you can build things with your hands, you have a responsibility as a Christian to be *building* up your life (v. 20). Other passages in Scripture talk about building our life on our faith as well. 1 Corinthians 3:11 assures us that as believers we have a solid foundation, and Jesus says in Matthew 7 that if you will listen to and obey His teachings, you will be a *wise builder*, as compared to an unwise builder who doesn't count the cost or build on a solid foundation. A well constructed house or life is a beautiful sight as well as very functional. **What kind of life are you building for yourself? Are you using the right foundation? Would God say it was both beautiful and functional?**

QuietTime

Do you like stories that have happy endings? This week we will see how God changes tragedy into triumph!

WEEK 53

Prayer focus for this week

THE QUESTION · *What is the writer saying?*
THE ANSWER · *How Can I apply this to my life?*

Sunday · RUTH 1:1-14

DIGGING DEEPER · God used famine either to test the faithfulness of Israel or to chastise her for sin, the latter being the case here. Elimelech, Naomi, and their two sons, Mahlon and Chilion, left Bethlehem, "the house of bread and praise," to go into the land of the Moabites. These people were antagonistic to the Israelites and worshiped idols. Mahlon and Chilion married Moabite women after their father died. Their names were Orpah and Ruth. After a short time the two sons died, leaving Naomi, Orpah and Ruth as childless widows. With no heir to carry on the family name, Naomi feels like the Lord is against her and decides to return to Bethlehem alone. Orpah returns to her family and her idols, but Ruth stays with Naomi.

Ever felt all alone like Naomi (Matthew 28:20)? What can you do when you feel lonely (Isaiah 40:31)? Why do you think Orpah returned to her gods?

Monday · RUTH 1:15-22

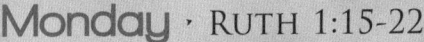

DIGGING DEEPER · About 10 years have passed and it is springtime. Ruth is determined to return with Naomi to Bethlehem, both of them as poor widows. Ruth makes a vow to Naomi to follow her, live where she lives, die and be buried where she does, and to worship her God. When Naomi comes into town she is recognized by many of the townspeople. She tells the people that her name should no longer be Naomi, meaning *pleasant*, but Mara, meaning *bitter*…because she feels that the Lord has dealt bitterly with her.

Do you think God ever treats people unfairly? Do you think that Ruth wanted to go with Naomi because of Naomi's testimony? What kind of testimony do you have?

Tuesday · RUTH 2:1-12

DIGGING DEEPER · Even though she was unaware of the Jewish laws, Ruth asked permission of Naomi to go and glean from the fields so that they would have something to eat. By law she had this right. To "glean" is to go behind the reapers in a field and pick up the kernels of grain left by the reapers. Ruth unknowingly chooses a field that belongs to a wealthy kinsman (relative) of Naomi, by the name of Boaz. He asks her to glean in his field, assuring her of water and protection. He has also heard of her good reputation.

Why do you think that Naomi didn't mention the Jewish laws to Ruth? Do you see any similarity between the protection and the offering of water by Boaz and what Jesus offers the believer?

Wednesday · RUTH 2:13-23

Q

A

DIGGING DEEPER • After thanking Boaz for his kindness, Ruth is offered lunch with the reapers. After lunch, Boaz instructs his reapers to allow larger portions of the grain to fall and also to let Ruth glean among the reapers. At the end of the day she thrashes out her gleanings and has nearly a half-bushel of grain—more than a normal amount. Naomi realizes that something special has taken place. Learning that it is because of Boaz, Naomi tells Ruth that he is a kinsman and that he has displayed signs of being willing to be a kinsman redeemer (Deuteronomy 25:5). Ruth spends over two months gleaning in Boaz's fields.

Do you think Ruth has trusted in the "Lord God of Israel"? Why do you think Boaz was showing special favors toward Ruth?

Thursday · RUTH 3:1-18

Q

A

DIGGING DEEPER • Naomi becomes a "matchmaker." The word *rest* indicates security of marriage (v. 1). Naomi explains some of the Jewish law concerning a kinsman redeemer. Her instructions to Ruth would encourage Ruth to be more aggressive in her approach toward Boaz. This was perfectly within the confines of Levitical law (Deuteronomy 25:5, 7-10). In verse 9, *spread thy skirt* is a request for protection and a promise of marriage. No impropriety is intended or takes place during this meeting. Boaz's response is that he is willing to be the kinsman redeemer, but there is a closer relative who must be offered this position before Boaz is even eligible. At this moment Boaz is concerned with preserving Ruth's virtue.

How do you react when other people's customs are different than yours? Why should Boaz be concerned about Ruth's virtue (Proverbs 12:4)?

Friday · RUTH 4:1-12

Q

A

DIGGING DEEPER • The "city gates" were used much like our courthouses. All city government and legal matters were handled at the gates. Boaz brings the other kinsman before ten elders who act as witnesses. The kinsman is interested in purchasing until he finds out that he would also have to marry and support Ruth. This would interfere with his own inheritance. By his actions, he passes on to Boaz the right to be the kinsman redeemer. Boaz claims the land, and Ruth as his wife. The witnesses all offer Boaz a blessing on him, Ruth, and their home.
Why did Boaz go through this process before claiming the land and Ruth for his own? Do you follow the laws and customs of today? What laws have you broken?

Saturday · RUTH 4:13-22

Q

A

DIGGING DEEPER • Ruth becomes the wife of Boaz, and God blesses them with a child. The women of Bethlehem name the child Obed, and assure Naomi that God has blessed her with a daughter-in-law who loves her and is better than seven sons. Naomi is very pleased and becomes a nurse to the child. More than likely, she no longer feels that she has been dealt with bitterly. Obed becomes the grandfather of King David (v. 22). But more significantly, he is in the lineage of the King of Kings... Jesus (Matthew 1:1-16), who was born in this same little town of Bethlehem (Matthew 2:1).
How do you feel when someone else receives a blessing? Why did the women think that Ruth was better to Naomi than seven sons (v. 15)? Do you see a similarity between Jesus and Boaz? Explain your answer.

The following chart is provided to enable everyone using Word of Life Quiet Times to stay on the same passages. This list also aligns with the daily radio broadcasts.

week 1	Aug 24 – Aug 30	Psalms 51:1-56:13
week 2	Aug 31 – Sep 6	Psalms 57:1-63:11
week 3	Sep 7 – Sep 13	Psalms 64:1-68:35
week 4	Sep 14 – Sep 20	Psalms 69:1-72:11
week 5	Sep 21 – Sep 27	Psalms 72:12-76:12
week 6	Sep 28 – Oct 4	1 Timothy 1:1-4:8
week 7	Oct 5 – Oct 11	1 Timothy 4:9-6:21
week 8	Oct 12 – Oct 18	Leviticus 1:1-23:14
week 9	Oct 19 – Oct 25	Leviticus 23:15-26:46
week 10	Oct 26 – Nov 1	Mark 1:1-3:12
week 11	Nov 2 – Nov 8	Mark 3:13-5:20
week 12	Nov 9 – Nov 15	Mark 5:21-7:13
week 13	Nov 16 – Nov 22	Mark 7:14-9:29
week 14	Nov 23 – Nov 29	Mark 9:30-11:11
week 15	Nov 30 – Dec 6	Mark 11:12-13:23
week 16	Dec 7 – Dec 13	Mark 13:24-14:65
week 17	Dec 14 – Dec 20	Mark 14:66-16:20
week 18	Dec 21 – Dec 27	1 John 1:1-2:27
week 19	Dec 28 – Jan 3	1 John 2:28-4:21
week 20	Jan 4 – Jan 10	1 John 5:1 - 3 John 14
week 21	Jan 11 – Jan 17	Ezra 1:1-5:5
week 22	Jan 18 – Jan 24	Ezra 5:6-8:36
week 23	Jan 25 – Jan 31	Ezra 9:1 - Haggai 2:23
week 24	Feb 1 – Feb 7	Nehemiah 1:1-4:23
week 25	Feb 8 – Feb 14	Nehemiah 5:1-13:14
week 26	Feb 15 – Feb 21	Acts 1:1-3:11